MW00855992

RISK. FAIL. RISE.

M. COLLEEN CRUZ

RISK. FAIL. RISE.

A Teacher's Guide to Learning from Mistakes

HEINEMANN Portsmouth, NH

Heinemann

361 Hanover Street

Portsmouth, NH 03801-3912

www.heinemann.com

Offices and agents throughout the world

The author and publisher wish to thank those who have generously given permission to reprint borrowed material:

Figure I-4 from *Lifelong Kindergarten: Cultivating Creativity Through Projects, Passion, Peers, and Play* by Mitchel Resnick. Copyright © 2017 by Mitchel Resnick. Published by MIT Press. Reprinted by permission of the author.

Acknowledgments for borrowed material continue on p. 135.

Library of Congress Cataloging-in-Publication Data
Name: Cruz, Maria Colleen, author.
Title: Risk. Fail. Rise. : a teacher's guide to learning from mistakes / M. Colleen Cruz.
Description: First Edition. | Portsmouth, NH : Heinemann, 2020. | Includes bibliographical references.
Identifiers: LCCN 2020033798 | ISBN 9780325112473
Subjects: LCSH: Effective teaching. | Motivation in education. | Teacher-student relationships. | Classroom management.
Classification: LCC LB1025.3 .C79 2020 | DDC 371.102—dc23
LC record available at https://lccn.loc.gov/2020033798

Editor: Margaret LaRaia
Production: Vicki Kasabian
Interior and cover designs: Suzanne Heiser
Cover image: © Getty Images/discan (*burst graphic*)
Interior photos: © Shutterstock/Vitalii Vodolazskyi (*crumpled paper background*); © Getty Images/Jenner Images (*origami bird*)
Author photo: Nadine Baldasare
Typesetting: Kim Arney
Manufacturing: Steve Bernier/Valerie Cooper

Printed in the United States of America on acid-free paper
1 2 3 4 5 6 7 8 9 10 VP 25 24 23 22 21 20
September 2020 Printing

For New York City,

which has taught so many of us about

risk, failure, and still managing to

rise

Contents

Acknowledgments

This book was written over several years, working with lots of different schools, districts and communities. It is also deeply personal, and my gratitude goes way beyond the usual professional contacts and close family.

First and foremost, I am grateful to Lucy Calkins, my friend and most influential mentor. Her generosity, knowledge, and vulnerability have been a guiding force in my work for a long time. This book stands on the shoulders of the Teachers College Reading and Writing Project, the organization Lucy leads and my professional home. The organization's greatest strength is and always has been its people. During the years this book was being written, the organization has dealt with some of the toughest challenges it has ever faced with grace, honesty, and a dedication to keeping children's well-being always at the forefront. I am profoundly grateful to be a part of this organization and am particularly grateful to the TCRWP leaders: Laurie Pessah, Mary Ehrenworth, Amanda Hartman, and Emily Butler-Smith. I am also thankful for all of the support and brainstorming offered by TCRWP staff developers, including my "ride-or-die" Natalie Louis, the straight-shooting Brooke Gellar, my friend in books Katy Wischow, and the always brilliant Shana Frazin.

I thank all of the many schools I have worked with, sharing ideas for this book, piloting concepts, and sometimes just pushing pack. A special thank-you goes to the American School in Paris, P.S. 116, P.S. 118, P.S. 176, P.S. 130, P.S. 29, The Special Music School, Springs Elementary, and Roosevelt Elementary. Another special thank-you goes to Hewlett Elementary for being my longtime thought partners and for trying out many of the earliest iterations of the concepts in this book. I thank the final pilot teachers: Kerri Hook, Connie Pertuz-Mesa, and Sarah Scheldt, whose students' work informs this book.

I am incredibly grateful to the brilliant and powerful Sonja Cherry-Paul. My person and my work have become exponentially stronger because of her. I am also grateful to Jennifer Serravallo for being my constant friend, thought partner, and bouncing board and to

Kate Roberts for her enduring friendship and special commiseration skills. I thank Maggie Roberts for her thoughtful insights and constant cheerleading. And, as always, I am very grateful to my Wednesday Night Writing group, my writing community that keeps me grounded in the connections between writing and love.

I cannot thank enough two of the early readers of this book, Chris Hass and Arlène Casimir. Their insights and notes on this book were invaluable. I am also thankful to Ali-yah Kjeldson Harrell for helping wrangle the many references throughout the book.

I am grateful to the entire team at Heinemann for their constant support and care throughout. I am thankful to Vicki Boyd and Roderick Spelman for their candid and open-hearted support and leadership. Thank you to Krysten Lebel and Sarah Fournier for organizing the materials for book production, Vicki Kasabian for turning a Word Doc into the physical book you now have in your hands, Suzanne Heiser for making the book's looks match its content, and Elizabeth Silvis for making sure people know it exists. A huge, endless amount of gratitude is being currently backed up in a tanker truck to the door of Margaret LaRaia, editor extraordinaire. It's been both a thrill and totally exhausting to be pushed further than I thought I could go by one of the smartest people I know. All of the best parts of this book are because of Margaret.

Finally, the biggest thank-yous of all go to my family. It could not have been easy to be living your life with a person constantly studying every mistake you make, and a chunk of that while in quarantine! Thank you to my constant fans and personal promotion team, Joan and Will Cruz. I am grateful to my brother Mike for his unshakeable support and calm. Thank you to Nico Cruz for reminding me to stop and play every day and to Sam Cruz for the endless hours getting lost in books and words together. To Charlie Cruz, my dog muse, who could be found curled up at my feet while I worked late into the night. But most of all I am grateful to Nadine Baldasare, who made it possible for me to survive this wacky-entirely-too-much-to-do year with her unwavering support, humor, and always enough time to share a glass of wine and a story.

Introduction

These Brains Are Made for Mistaking

Much to my mother's chagrin, I have never been a perfectionist.

Whether it was cleaning the bathroom, checking my spelling, or placing a bumper sticker straight, I've always been comfortable with the little errors and slips that occur on a daily basis. I am proudly and profoundly imperfect. It's become as much of a part of my identity as my pessimism or my love of Brooklyn or being a mom. To double down, I collect little catchphrases about this embrace of imperfection and have for a long time. If you've hung out with me at all, you've likely heard me quote any of the following:

> "Good enough for government work!"—*not sure who said it first, but picked it up from my high school chemistry teacher, Mr. Flint*

> "Done is better than perfect."—*from a poster Sheryl Sandberg has in her office*

> "When you decide that you want to be brave, it opens up way more possibilities than trying to be perfect ever does."—*Alexandria Ocasio-Cortez*

Most of the other educators I know also embrace some sort of imperfectionism. If you're holding this book you probably do too. You believe, and probably say to your students, that mistakes are a natural part of learning. And, of course, this is true. But how much do your curricular choices, teaching methods, and student behaviors reflect this belief? After all, you're not the first teacher, nor will you be the last, who has talked to their students about how true learning is an imperfect process. As I saw how little our classrooms reflect this belief, I started to wonder if perhaps we're all just paying lip service to an idea that we haven't yet created systems to support.

Learn from mistakes - show learning by redo / retake

Difference between feedback / grading

Math controversy — Glad you gave that answer because many make the same mistakes

Mistakes part of the process but not the ultimate goal (J. Boaler seems to embrace the mistakes more than the correct solutions to the math)

I know this has been true for me in my work as an educator. We all talk a lot about mistakes, but if we're honest, we don't find ourselves or our students truly embracing mistakes practically and visibly on a regular basis. Digging into the research, habits, and expectations educators have about mistakes, I've gained a greater awareness of the contrast between what so many of us practice when it comes to mistakes and what we say. Maybe the most significant example of this is that we tell kids we value mistakes, but at the end of every marking period they are judged on those very things we tell them not to worry about. Recently I got into a huge discussion with a group of teachers across grade levels who were grappling with this issue. All agreed that they valued growth mindset and the importance of kids feeling free to take risks and make errors on the way to learning. But they all also owned that students who made fewer errors got higher grades. And with so many schools shifting to digital grading systems where students and their caregivers can check out their regular, often daily, grades, the real-time consequences of taking a learning risk is something that very much might result in accusations thrown across the dinner table. The teachers were concerned about the disconnect between the words they said in class each day about risk-taking and the very real-world consequences of getting a bad grade in the grading portal. "There's a big difference between feedback and grading, but the system we're using isn't really differentiating that."

Conversations like these made me realize that we as educators need better models of practice on mistake-making. Although we might not yet be able to change our district grading systems, we can still create space for mistake-making in our classrooms. This book is my effort to share what research studies say on mistake-making as part of learning and what that means for our teaching.

Unintentional Mistakes We Can Learn From

It's always important to have a working definition of whatever topic you're studying. The term *mistake* covers a wide range of behaviors, from intentional to unintentional harm. I suspect that the broad definition is part of the reason speaking about mistakes can be such slippery work. To avoid that, I've chosen to delineate between the word *mistake* and purposeful wrongdoing, or as the Catholic-raised me might call it, sin. Too often we hear famous people apologize for their "mistake" of embezzling, having an affair, or lying. Or we cajole a student into admitting to the "mistake" of punching someone in the face, cheating on a test, or vandalizing the bathrooms. Those are all examples of what I would call wrongdoing. When the person acted, they knew what they were doing was wrong but chose to do it anyway, even if it was for a seemingly justified reason.

A mistake happens by accident: I meant to turn in the attendance list, but I forgot. A wrongdoing or sin happens mindfully: I knew it was wrong to take home the toilet paper from the teacher's bathroom, but I did it anyway. It is very rare for someone to *accidentally* end up stealing. Just because the active party might be filled with regret in both accidental and intentional mistakes, the rationale and ways to repair and grow are very different. It seems to me that one of the (many) reasons there is so much shame and denial attached to garden variety mistakes is that too often purposeful wrongdoing and mistakes are conflated. Even though those terms are often used interchangeably, I want to bring light to our unconsciousness around some mistakes in schools and so will focus on mistakes in their accidental form. Mindful wrongdoing will need to go in another book.

In the essays and lessons in this book, when we talk about mistakes, we'll concentrate on errors, missteps, and blunders—situations where the teacher or student had the intention to do one thing but ended up doing something else. The intention and outcome were different—whether tripping on the stairs, miscalculating a math problem, or giving the wrong year for a historical event. The point is that awareness sharpens intention and improves outcomes. Of course, we can't achieve perfect awareness. Sometimes the mistake-maker knows right away that a mistake was made (breaking the *e* key by pressing too hard). Sometimes the mistake-maker doesn't know until later (the envelope gets returned because there's no stamp). And sometimes the mistake is never discovered. Sometimes it is only after making a mistake that we realize we had a whole bunch of intentions we weren't even aware of (Hello, wrong name on the email that made me aware I intended that note to feel personal and not cut and pasted!). But the more aware we are of why we make certain mistakes and what we can do to improve situations once we've made them, the more effective our teaching and learning will be.

And let's acknowledge that not every environment makes it safe to focus on learning from our mistakes. Even though mistake-making is part of learning, in our current climate in schools, mistakes can sometimes feel complicated to discuss and define in honest ways. The work of this book is to try to get us past that. If we can create school cultures where we talk honestly about mistakes, then we can grow and create opportunities for children to grow in all the ways they deserve. And we deserve those opportunities too.

Why People Make Mistakes

Mistakes, like most things humans do, are both impossibly unique and boringly predictable. When looking across your typical day in school, you've likely done or witnessed a whole slew of mistakes: yelling out the wrong answer, accusing the wrong kid of goofing off, misspelling a word, inaccurately measuring the materials for an experiment, leaving the intercom on when the announcements are through. Our responses to mistakes are largely affected by whether or not we committed them, if they were committed against us, or if we merely observed them. Often, our forgiveness hinges on whether we're the victim or not. In his explanation of the difference between tragedy and comedy, Mel Brooks implies this: "Tragedy is when I break a fingernail. Comedy is when you fall into an open sewer and die" (Byrne 2012, 78). The less affected we are by the mistake, the more we're able to have a good sense of humor, empathy, and an ability to dispassionately study mistakes. For that reason, active study of mistakes before they happen, and of past mistakes, can help distance personal egos enough to lay the groundwork for a mistake-welcoming school culture.

When we create space for that more objective distance, we can study the common reasons we make mistakes. Kathryn Schulz in her book *Being Wrong: Adventures in the Margin of Error* (2011) offers useful categories of how mistakes start.

Take a moment and hold in your mind a recent mistake you made in school. Then, look at Schulz's list of origin of errors (see Figure I-1) to decide what was the catalyst(s) for your own.

Origin of Error	Teacher Examples
Our Senses—When we see, smell, taste, touch, or hear something we can be moved to action that turns out wrong.	We see a student in the hallway and are sure they should be in a classroom. We call out their name, only to realize as we get closer that they are not the same student we thought they were. A student responds to a question we ask in class and we snap at them because we think they said something snarky, but we just misheard.
Knowledge—Kathryn Schulz describes knowledge as "belief with citations." When we hold knowledge about something that turns out to not be accurate or it turns out we thought we knew something that we didn't.	We find ourselves toe to toe with a student, arguing in the middle of class because the student insisted that rats did not cause the black plague. We are absolutely taken aback that the student would question us so publicly and especially about something that was settled science. In a fit of anger, we turn to the internet in front of the class to prove our point, only to find out that there had actually been a couple of recently published studies on it. And although it hasn't been fully concluded that rats did not spread the black plague, it is no longer considered certain that they did. We immediately apologize and realize how powerful admitting our error can be to student engagement.

Origin of Error	Teacher Examples
Belief—So much of our actions are based on our beliefs rather than factual evidence.	We believe that is the school's policy so we enforce it. We believe a parent is angry at us so we go out of our way to win them over. We believe in someone's fixed nature so we make a decision about them. For example, we hear about a kid long before he is in our class. We've seen him in the halls and he's never smiling. We believe what other teachers have said and decide he's a bad kid and we don't want that kind of trouble in our classroom. But then he shows up. And once he gets there, we realize he's a kid who faces a lot of obstacles when trying to express himself in conversation or in writing. When he stumbles other kids mock him. When we give him tools to express himself, he gets friendlier and less disruptive. All at once we realize our belief is based on gossip and assumption.
Evidence—Sometimes we have some evidence. Hard facts about something. We then take action based on a conclusion that we are drawing based on very real evidence. Often when mistakes happen based on evidence, it is because we made an assumption.	A student isn't in our classroom. That's our first piece of evidence. We know an important midterm was scheduled for the day. Our second piece of evidence. When we ask the class if anyone knows the student's whereabouts, someone smirks. We look across our three pieces of evidence and assume they are skipping. We find out later they were sick in the nurse's office, waiting to be picked up and taken home. I find mistakes based off real evidence some of the hardest to cope with. There is something so alluring about evidence, so concrete that it is easy to forget that we are still making assumptions that could lead to mistakes.
Society—Often we make decisions because they are what society—writ large or small—expects or is doing. Society can be a country, city, neighborhood, or school.	When everyone in the English department assigns an hour a night of homework, we do too it because it's what society says is right. Even if we might have a funny feeling about it, even if we don't think our kids really need it. Then, later we find out every other department is doing the same thing and kids are buckling under four hours of homework a night. Deciding to correct this type of mistake can be harder than most because we now have to not only own responsibility for our errors, but we are in effect, by changing, suggesting that our colleagues are mistaken. The pressure for colleagues to support each other is real and logical; however, when colleagues are wrong it can be difficult to navigate that path.

continues

Origin of Error	Teacher Examples
The Allure of Certainty—All of us hold things that we are absolutely certain we are right about. Whether it's morality or culture or facts, there are things we know for sure, without a shadow of doubt that we are right about. We act on these things on a daily basis. That's because it feels great to know we are right. And yet, we intellectually know there are few things in life we can truly be certain about.	So when we get a student who meets all the class deadlines, whose work is neat, and who is respectful and seemingly engaged in lessons, we are certain they are a strong student and will be one of our highest performers. We treat them as such, and when deciding who to meet with during work time, we don't choose them because they seem to be doing well. However, when the first high-stakes assignment is due, we realize we were wrong. The student is dutiful, but their knowledge of the unit topic is shallow at best, confused at worst. This is not a matter of giving all students the benefit of the doubt and assuming greatness until proven otherwise. This is a situation where we zeroed in on this student and were sure they were one of the strongest students. So sure were we that we didn't even really study our own initial evaluations.

Figure I-1 Origin of Errors in School

Schulz's categories of origin of error allow us that necessary distance to recognize how things might have gone otherwise. When we're more aware, we can disrupt some of our brains' mistake-making inclinations. When I ask teachers and students to reflect on this, I start with a video. (It's one you might have seen before with an important twist in the plot line.) I reference this video a lot because the ending surprises students (and grown-ups), even though there are clues all along.

It's called *Snack Attack* (2015).

After the video, most of the students share their requisite shock. I gather them close in a sort of conspiratorial way—indicating I'm about to tell something important and rare.

"I want to let you know something really important," I say. "Something I never knew when I was your age and wish I did.

"I think you have heard the adage, 'Everyone makes mistakes.'" Students usually nod. "But what you might not have heard is that there are some predictable reasons why we make these mistakes. Most if not all of us made a small, low-stakes mistake just now while watching that video. But we might not all know why. Knowing why we make mistakes can help us make fewer mistakes and ensure that when we do make mistakes they'll be more of the more useful variety."

I display a chart with the types of mistakes. Depending on the age of the students, I might share Schulz's language. If they are younger, I might use something similar to Figure I-2.

Reasons We Make Mistakes

- We think we're right.

- We are focused on the wrong things.

- We think we know something we do not.

- We believe something wrong.   — *hesitancy to show wrong things in class because thi*

- Our senses are wrong.

- Our community expects us to take certain actions.

- We look to the wrong evidence.

Figure I-2 **Reasons We Make Mistakes**

"Watching that video, I think all of us probably could point to one, if not more than one, thing we did that created the opportunity for us to make our mistake and not see what was really happening with the cookies. Like, I was *making assumptions* about the kid with the headphones, so I didn't even think twice about any other possible explanation. Or, maybe you felt like the whole class was in on the joke of how angry the woman was getting and how much the teenager didn't seem to care and were enjoying laughing together (*community*). Or, maybe you were gathering *evidence* that you thought was pointing to his guilt, like how he ate the cookies and wiped the crumbs off her lap. But that same evidence was actually showing how kind he was.

"I find it interesting to study any inaccurate assumptions I made and to reflect on whether those are some of my regular mistake-making habits. Like, do I tend to focus on the wrong things a lot? When I tend to go with the crowd or community, do I tend to make mistakes? Or, am I so in love with being right, that even though I could be wrong, I still make choices that lead to mistakes?" I use first person here because, before I ask them to think about themselves, I want them to see that making mistakes is shared by us all, adults and kids.

"I'd like you to think about a personal mistake you made recently. I know that's hard because often we don't even realize when we made a mistake. So it might have to be one that ended badly—that you know for a fact it was a mistake. It doesn't have to be big or terrible. Just a mistake. Now, with a partner, talk over that mistake and see if you can tease out what the cause was. If you have a few more minutes, think about another time you made a different mistake for similar reasons. And remember, the point of the conversation isn't to judge each other for our mistakes but to support each other in thinking about them."

After the students talk, I might then take that lesson to whatever subject area they are working on at the moment. If I were teaching a lesson in mathematics, I might ask the students to go through past problems they worked on and find out if the origins of their mistakes are ever repeated. Perhaps they kept using an algorithm they thought was right for a problem, but was actually a mismatch (*misunderstanding/misconception*). Or maybe they rushed through their calculations, but because they're only focused on the steps to the problem, they don't think to double check their calculations (*focus*).

No matter the discipline, if students are learning within their zone of proximal development, they should have at least a handful of recent errors—enough to help them identify a pattern that will allow them to study whether or not their errors tend to stem from a certain origin. The most important work this activity does is set up the larger idea that mistake-making is part of what the human brain does. Mistakes are, in and of themselves, not the problem. The shame we attach to mistakes and unwillingness to grow from them is.

Freedom to Make Mistakes Means Freedom to Grow

As I said earlier, some of the research around mistake-making might surprise you. Here's one example: a study out of the University of Texas Medical Branch at Galveston (UTMB Newsroom 2012) found that when high school sophomores who played video games were pitted against surgical residents in a surgical simulation, the gamers did better than the surgical residents. What?! I was skeptical but through further reading I discovered that this study had been replicated in a few different ways over the years. The studies go on to show that not only do video gamers do better with surgical simulations, but actual surgeons, if they played video games at least three hours per week, performed surgeries with 37 percent fewer errors than other surgeons. Additionally, and perhaps the most surprising to me, was that if surgeons played select video games just prior to surgery, they performed faster and with fewer errors (Rosser et al. 2007).

There are of course several different reasons this might be the case, the most obvious among them, of course, is that video game players would have great eye-hand coordination and reaction time due to the nature of playing fast-paced games.

But, as we look more closely, we also see that regular video game players are more likely to be flexible thinkers and better able to deal with stress (Gee 2007; Gray 2012), which I interpret to mean that people who play video games not only get repeated access to opportunities to make mistakes, but due to the immediate nature of video game feedback, get an opportunity to study those mistakes and immediately learn from them.

I admit that this feels counterintuitive; after all, when we think of surgeons, we talk about surgical precision. We think of being error-free. Nobody wants a neurosurgeon who has a .165 batting average. We want someone with a 1.000. But what if the thing that makes that possible is exactly the opposite? In other words, it is entirely possible that what makes a surgeon capable of exacting perfection is lots and lots of opportunities to make mistakes. Frequently and recently. That's where video games come in. They create mortality-free opportunities to get regular and frequent opportunities to take chances and make mistakes.

How many of us have felt that students are disengaged because they play too many video games? Could it be instead that video games are fun and cognitively and emotionally rewarding in a way that school often isn't? With video games, players get plenty of opportunities to take simulated risks and make mistakes with low or no consequences, what growth mindset expert and cofounder of Growth Mindset Works (with Carol Dweck) Eduardo Briceño (2016) would call the *Learning Zone*. He differentiates the learning zone from the *Performance Zone*. The performance zone where we apply our skills and try to do the best work we can to show what we are capable of. The learning zone is where we practice, experiment, take risks, and expect to make low-risk mistakes on our way to learning. Video games live firmly in this world of low-stake risk and skills learned by repeated practice. They are in a realm that is in sharp contrast to the assignment-grading treadmill many students experience in school, where we put them in a position similar to surgeons, where they are expected to learn through high-cost errors, what Briceño would call the performance zone.

The idea of mistake-making when it comes to surgeons is horrifying. None of us want to be on the table under the scalpel of a surgeon who is taking risks and knows the chances are good they'll make a mistake. Which is precisely why I'm using this example. Because for all of our desire to steer clear of mistake-making surgeons, we also know that mistakes are necessary for surgical training. Even though so many of our best medical developments happened after a mistake was made, most of us would still rather avoid being the recipient of said mistakes. And yet, without mistakes we'd be missing quite a bit. What writer Barney Saltzberg (2010) calls "the beautiful oops" has led, throughout human history, to some pretty essential learning. Let's stick with the medical example for a minute and look at how mistakes and a certain mindset about mistake-making resulted in some life-saving discoveries. See Figure I–3.

Mistake that led to . . .	This medical innovation
The story goes that Alexander Fleming was studying staph infections and feeling salty because one of his lab assistants had been moved to another lab. So he left his dirty petri dishes in the sink and went on vacation. While he was gone, a penicillium mold spore somehow flew in through a window or from somewhere and landed in one of his staph petri dishes. When he came back, the petri dishes that had been accidentally exposed to penicillium were clean and the staph infection gone.	Penicillin for treatment of infectious diseases
Karl Paul Link was studying why cows were bleeding and discovered their spoiled clover feed was part of the problem. Mark Strahmann then narrowed down which element of their spoiled clover feed caused that bleeding and then isolated that element. It was then marketed as rat poison. However, when a Navy recruit attempted suicide with the new rat poison and survived, it was discovered it could be used for humans as a blood thinner.	Warfarin—which started the use of oral anticoagulants—or blood thinners, which are used to help reduce the risk of blood clotting and help treat certain types of heart diseases
F. Mason Sones, a cardiologist, was using dye to check the valves and chambers of a patient when the catheter he was using slipped and he accidentally injected dye into the patient's coronary artery. The doctor thought he had killed the patient, only to discover the patient was fine and, because he could now also see the patient's coronary artery, he realized he had discovered a new way of cardiac imaging and surgery.	Coronary angiogram
Wilson Greatbatch was working on an oscillator that could record heartbeats. He put in a wrong part, but soon realized that the mechanism was pulsing, like a heart.	The pacemaker—which stimulates the heart muscle to create a regular heartbeat

Figure I-3 **The Opportunity to Make and Learn from Mistakes**

Although it's true that much of the time teachers are not dealing with life-and-death mistake-making, we are often charged with responsibilities that will have a direct impact on the types of lives our students will live. If our students do not learn to read, it will be difficult if not impossible for them to get a decent salaried job when they leave school. If our students do not learn critical thinking skills and cannot spot untrue or biased information, they might make misinformed health decisions such as choosing not to vaccinate their children or have their vote swayed by online propaganda. If our students do not feel like school is reflective or welcoming to their identities and backgrounds, they might decide education is not for them altogether and underperform or drop out. The list of ways school has a direct and lasting impact on people's lives is never-ending. And that can feel like an impossible level of pressure. We might be tempted to hand over all our decision-making to a packaged program or curriculum or something we purchased from another teacher online or perhaps even a social media site. We might be tempted to just do exactly what we have done for the last five, ten, thirty years, even if we know there is undoubtedly more current and successful approaches to try. Many of us walk into our classrooms virtually frozen from concern of making mistakes.

This not only reduces our ability to be responsive to our current students' needs and to innovate, it also models something quite dangerous to our students—that safe and possibly irrelevant work is better than risky, relevant (and likely messy) work. Certainly that's an argument for why we need to create more space for creative failure in our classrooms. Let's look at a different video game example to see what we can pull from that to do so.

My family has a Nintendo Switch. Recently I was playing a Mario game for *way* too long. I knew it was too long. I had laundry to do. Lessons to plan. But I just kept playing this one level, dying and then starting over and over again. Usually when I tell students this story they nod and laugh. As I kept playing the game while my work piled up, I realized that what was making me keep playing this game was not that I was doing so well, it was that *I kept making mistakes*. Some of the mistakes were the same, but a lot of them were new each time I played.

Mistakes are part of what makes video games fun, but somehow in life, if I was making as many mistakes as I was making on that one level of Mario, I would have quit whatever I was doing. It was the mistakes that kept me going—the feeling that if I just did it right this time, I would be successful. I have noticed something interesting about myself and other video game players, or at least interesting to me: when a level is mastered quickly, it is very easy to turn off the game. Play just a few rounds and let it go. But, when the player is close to accomplishing something but then makes a mistake, it can feel almost impossible to stop.

That feeling of being so close to mastering something, of seeing that I had *almost* nailed it, that incredible impetus that propelled me forward, to want to keep pushing, is exactly what educators long to see more of in our classrooms. That sort of good-natured, but very much determined, acceptance of errors as a welcome and expected part of learning would help propel all of students' learning, no matter what discipline we teach, to the next level. We'll explore ways of making that happen in this book, but for this work to be honest and responsible, I want to keep honoring how difficult mistake-making can feel for teachers right now.

Mistake-Making as a Mindful Practice

Recently I was fortunate to have a conversation with Mitchel Resnick, creator of Scratch, MIT professor, and author of *Lifelong Kindergarten* (2017), about mistakes and creativity. As part of our conference day for teachers at Teachers College Reading and Writing Project, we, along with another colleague of mine, Sara Berg, were planning to ask teachers to take part in a makerspace. I raised the concern that when I'd run makerspaces in the past with educators, I saw a fair amount of hesitation before they were willing to jump in and play with the materials. We discussed how often this was out of fear of screwing things up.

Resnick (2017) talked about a Creative Learning Spiral as a way of exploring the process of creativity (see Figure I-4). He discussed the ways in which play, or tinkering, and reflection were key aspects of that process. And how often he found the older we are, the more hesitant we can be at tinkering. He talked about how the fear we have of making mistakes can be a huge hinderance because mistake-making is a crucial part of the creative process. And this process doesn't just help us in terms of the projects we are working on at the moment. The habit of mistake-making and reflection are habits that serve us well in all aspects of our lives. As Resnick writes in *Lifelong Kindergarten,* "There's a tradition among programmers to see mistakes not as a sign of failure but as 'bugs' that can be fixed. An important part of becoming a programmer is to learn strategies

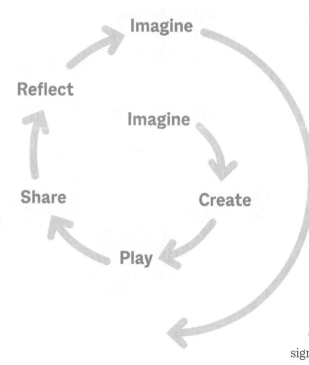

Figure I-4 Creative Learning Spiral

for debugging—that is, how to identify and isolate a problem, then make changes to get around the problem." In other words, by actively expecting and responding to mistakes we are also honing and practicing important skills and strategies that might not be developed or practiced any other way.

When I think about preparing for positive risk-taking that will embrace certain types of mistake-making, something I explored in *Unstoppable Writing Teacher* (2015) comes to mind—research suggests that pessimists are often happier and healthier than optimists, an idea that often comes as a shock to people. Research also suggests that optimists are happier and healthier, but this is less shocking to most. The healthy pessimist does surprise because people see pessimists as gloomy and under a rain cloud. But really, pessimism is less about feeling worried all the time and more about preparation for difficulty—because we anticipate trouble. When we go into the world, we expect trouble and we plan for it. I think this extends into and includes mistake-making, whether or not you identify as a pessimist. If I am about to take a risk as an educator, or encourage my students to take a risk, it feels important to anticipate trouble. What might get in the way of success? What kinds of mistakes can I anticipate I might make?

A few years ago, Lucy Calkins, the founding director of the Teachers College Reading and Writing Project, gave a talk about trouble. She said something that I have been turning in my mind ever since: "We are all made up of a mix of achievements and failures. But our achievements, even the ones we are most proud of, are sort of generic. They can be anyone's achievements. Our achievements are not what make us unique. Our failures, on the other hand, are. Our mistakes and what we learned and what we became because of them are uniquely us. They make us who we are. We are nothing without our failures."

I wrote this book because I want to harness the perseverance humans have when we are playing video games—when we welcome mistakes and are driven by them, in our schools and in classrooms. I want us to learn to see our mistakes as unique and telling about who we are as our DNA. In equal measure, I want us to get better at minimizing unnecessary mistakes that can cause real harm and setbacks to the learning process. Throughout the book I will point to research outside of education, in fields as varied as medicine, video game play, social work, architecture, and even the FDA. Yes, looking at research around learning and teaching is crucial, but I believe, in order to have a deep understanding of the role of risks, mistakes and responses, we also need to look outside our own field. In other words, as much as a firefighter's whole job is to take a risk and run toward the fire, they also value risk reduction as a means to allow themselves to continue to take more risks, I believe educators can do and teach in the same way. It's a balance I believe we can achieve. We recognize the risk and take it when we know the outcomes for ourselves and for our students are worth it.

Choose Your Own Adventure: A Note About Using This Book

I've called these essays rather than chapters because I really intend this to be a choose your own adventure kind of read. As every teacher knows, engagement makes all the difference in learning. When someone tries to control too much of your learning experience, the less the learning becomes your own. And to grow from our mistakes, we really need to bring our full attention to it. So, with that in mind, I wrote this book as a collection of essays that can be read out of order and in isolation. What kind of mistakes do you want to pay attention to right now? You decide.

MISTAKES COST MORE FOR SOME

According to Yudhijit Bhattacharjee (2017), we lie to achieve goals. Thirty-six percent of our lies stem from a desire to protect ourselves, and 44 percent of our lies are to promote ourselves. Compare that to the harsh reality that only 7 percent of our lies are to be polite or altruistic. As early as age four we begin to lie to avoid punishment (Bronson 2008). We know that one of the hardest times for us to stay honest is when we feel like someone is blaming or accusing us. It's the reason that, when we witness a kid punch another kid, we shouldn't ask, "Did you just punch him?" Because even though they know they were caught in action, the instinctive human response when we are asked to admit guilt is to deny it. It shouldn't be surprising that for so many of us, when observed making a mistake by another, we are defensive. We immediately look to protect ourselves. So, when the kid responds with "No, I didn't" and we say, "But I saw you do it!," their next self-protective move is to emphasize intent over impact: "They punched me first."

Publicly owning up to our mistakes involves fighting against our own instincts. I think it can be even harder for teachers to do than for the general population. After all, the teacher is supposed to be the expert. It feels daunting to imagine how students, families, administrators, and colleagues might respond to us admitting our mistakes. There could be a lack of respect or lack of trust in our abilities. However, if we are serious about the notion that one of the most important ways for people to learn is to take risks, we need to do more than pay mistake ownership lip service. We need to publicly practice it. Let's consider a recent example of what that looks like.

On a spring evening in 2019 at a Major League Baseball game in Houston, Albert Almora, a player for the Chicago Cubs, hit a foul ball. It went flying into the stands and crashed into a young girl's head. She was whisked away, tears streaming down her face, injured. She ended up being fine, but Almora was clearly shaken. He fell to his knees and cried. A security guard and teammates comforted him. Hitting a foul ball into the stands is an innocent and fairly common occurrence. Statistics (NBC News Chicago 2019) show that there are roughly fifty foul balls hit on average at Major League Baseball games. No one thought Almora intended to hit the little girl.

But that was not what was troubling Albert.

He didn't go into the defensive mode that so many of us go into when we make mistakes. He didn't explain how he "didn't mean to" or proclaim how it was somehow the little girl and her family's fault. Instead, the cameras, and later witness accounts, showed he went directly into regret and concern. He focused only on the impact. In an interview following the incident, Almora said, "As soon as I hit it, the first person I locked eyes on was her. God willing, I'll be able to have a relationship with this little girl for the rest of my life. But, um, just prayers right now. That's all I really can control. I'm speechless. I'm at a loss for words. Being the father of two boys, I want to put a net around the whole stadium. Ah, man. I don't know. I'm sorry."

Almora knew that taking responsibility for the impact of a mistake, especially when the victim is not the mistake-maker themselves, is what matters most. There was no reason to beat himself up for it. However, there were plenty of reasons to wish the outcome had been different. This desire—knowing that mistakes happen but also wishing for an outcome that didn't have victims—is something many educators can relate to.

Not All Mistakes Are Equal

When we talk about the high-risk mistakes or the mistakes that have more impact for those on the mistake's receiving end, we still need to hold onto the awareness that there is such a thing as "good" mistakes. Our fear of negative impact can't keep us frozen and passive. Instead, it's about maintaining awareness so that we avoid as much negative impact as possible and that we take responsibility when the unavoidable negative impact happens. Mistakes are necessary on our path to learning. Knowing that there are different types might feel like semantics, but I believe that knowledge helps reduce negative errors and increase and welcome the positive errors.

Just like botanists learn how to identify flora and fauna, astronomers learn how to identify celestial bodies, and grammarians learn how to identify parts of speech, folks who study mistakes can develop a type of expertise when we start to consider ways to identify mistakes. This is because, like all things we study, it is easier to engage in a focused inquiry when we have names for things. We can identify patterns, notice challenges, consider alternatives only when we can articulate what we are specifically discussing. Naming is powerful.

With naming also comes the ability to categorize, rank, and value. Eduardo Briceño (2015b) gives us useful categories for four types of mistakes. Two types are more negative and two types are more positive. See Figure 1–1.

- *Stretch mistakes:* These are the types of positive mistakes most teachers and grown-ups like to talk about. These are the mistakes we make when we're trying something hard. Like a new algorithm, a logic strategy, or a complicated pipette technique. We're moving out of our comfort zone; because we're trying something new, we don't exactly get it right the first time. These are the mistakes the motivational posters are about.

- *Aha moment mistakes:* These are positive mistakes we make when we don't have all the information, so we think we're doing the right thing, until it becomes really clear it is not the right thing. One typical example is just how similar sugar and salt look when you mix them up while baking. In the classroom, these can happen the first time we try to teach a new grade or lesson. We lean on what we have in our curriculum guides or what our colleagues tell us. But as we move through that first lesson on quadrilaterals, we realize that the prerequisite teaching on angles and congruence hasn't happened. Or at least the students haven't retained it. Aha moment mistakes are also a type that give us a big learning experience. But unlike stretch mistakes, where we don't yet have the mastery of something, our mistakes allow us to see our areas of ignorance.

- *Sloppy mistakes:* These are the minor villains in the mistake world, the ones we like to catch other people making and hate to be caught doing ourselves. These are the mistakes we make when we're doing something we should know how to do, but we lose concentration or take something for granted and make a silly mistake that we really should not have made. We rush heading out the door

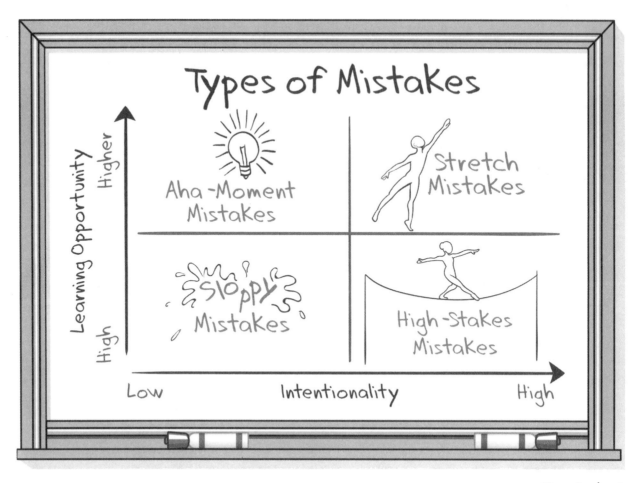

Figure 1-1 Types of Mistakes and Learning Opportunities

and leave our coffee on the counter. We give our students a long and elaborate lecture about personal responsibility and the importance of meeting academic demands after most of them failed to meet a key deadline, only to realize halfway through the lecture we are talking to the wrong class. Annoying. Low stakes. Easy to take ownership of.

- *High-stakes mistakes:* These are mistakes we really don't want to make. When the stakes are high, these types of mistakes can be life changing, or even cause physical harm. For example, when a parent asks us if we think they should have their child evaluated for possible services and we reflexively say no, but we almost instantly regret that response because we know the student is struggling too much with the content and suspect that there might be a learning disability. Yes, we can learn from these high-stakes mistakes, too, but these are also the mistakes we want to try to avoid making when we can. When we're in a high-stakes situation we want to do as much as possible to avoid mistakes. Education, like medicine and other first responder careers, is filled with high-stakes mistake pressure. We live each day knowing that our choices can make or break a child's ability to learn to read, reason, or reach their academic, career, or personal goals.

Knowing more about kinds of mistakes can help us to be more metacognitive about our mistakes. In the same way we learn a new digital skill or vocabulary word and then begin to see it everywhere, we will find ourselves more and more awake to the fumbles and downright mess-ups we (and others) make on a daily basis and understand that they do not all neatly fit into the same category. We can go into any learning situation expecting those stretch mistakes. We can identify situations that can result in high-stakes mistakes and do prep work to mitigate as much as possible the fallout from those types of mistakes.

Acknowledging Our Mistakes' Impacts on Students

A regular discussion in antiracist, equity-focused, social justice circles is about the tendency for those in power to own up to mistakes, only to quickly connect that mistake to intention (e.g., "I didn't intend to . . ."). This is such a big trope that even in some misguided trainings that deal with issues of race, class, ethnicity, gender, or other identities that are frequently marginalized, part of the protocols at the beginning for setting up conversational norms frequently includes the line, "Assume good intentions." And although it has the effect of making it less risky for the mistake-maker to apologize and still save face, it also has the effect of simultaneously allowing the mistake-maker to refuse to acknowledge harm done while chipping away at the victim's righteous indignation, and likely undermining the work being done.

So many of us do things that, while not at first glance harmful, have good intentions for people other than students. For example, who among us has not done something purely because we feel the need to be in compliance to some district or administrative dictate? We are doing _____ minutes of _____ because someone ordered us to, and not doing the _____ minutes of _____ that our students need. We make all the students use a particular form of note-taking because someone at the district office ordered it, while knowing full well this is going to not work as well for every kid. Or, another common choice we educators make is to take actions to keep students "under control" whether in the moment or systemically so that we get good evaluations. I have witnessed students being snapped at or having recess or electives taken away because of behavior that normally would be dealt with more instructionally, simply because a supervisor was in the room. The intent in those moments is to please the administration, not to do what's good for kids. And although this is completely understandable, it is also important to consider what our intent really is in those moments.

It should go without saying that if you are reading this book, your intent is good. And you are not going to make mistakes that intentionally hurt people. And your students very likely know your intent is good. And, yes, on occasion you *might* need to clarify that your intentions were on the right side of things. However, ideally, we all first check in with ourselves before doing so to make sure that we're not prioritizing our desire to feel good about ourselves over harm done to others. As Almora's example reminds us, making excuses or stating intentions does very little for the person wronged or the witness to the mistake. Our students and their families are most adversely impacted from our errors, intentional or not. As the maker of the mistake, the onus is on us to focus and acknowledge the impact. Sometimes the impact is small—"Oops, I spilled some water on your desk—let me wipe that up" and there's no need to declare "I didn't mean to spill water!" Sometimes the impact is big—mispronouncing a student's name for so long that other students are starting to joke about it. Our intention was not to marginalize this student or make them feel less valuable. But declaring our intention is not what the student needs. Instead, we should consider discussing the impact of our mistake, even if we're not entirely sure, but especially if we know. For example, we choose to say, "By mispronouncing your name for so long, and not taking the time to learn to pronounce it correctly, I might have sent the message that your name was somehow less important than other names. I also have noticed that some students have started to say it the way I have and I can only imagine how that makes you feel." Acknowledging impact helps everyone move forward (see Figure 1-2).

Bluntly acknowledging error might feel awkward, like you're fighting against your instincts. But it accomplishes important things. First, it takes care of anyone who might have been impacted by your mistake. Second, it models ownership of impact. This is of course important because students need to see lots of models of people taking ownership of their actions and their impact. We want them to take on those behaviors, but we also want them to trust us. When we own impact, we communicate that their relationship with us is about caring and respect. We will hold ourselves accountable to the relationship. When a person with authority does this, we communicate their value: that they have individual power and are deserving of respect. They have the right to expect people to take responsibility for the mistakes that have affected them. Particularly, but not only, mistakes made by those in power. Purposefully or not, by not acknowledging our errors we make with

Mistake Scenario	Language to Acknowledge Impact
You receive an email from a family that their child has reported you don't like them based on a recent class incident, and they would like to discuss this with you. You know you have been having trouble connecting with this student but thought your feelings weren't obvious.	"I am so glad you emailed to share your concern. If that's how <student's name> feels, then clearly there's work I need to do. It's important to me that I have a positive relationship with every child in my class. I'll bring greater attention to this and, in addition, I'd love to set up a time to talk with you about <child's name> so that I can get to know them better. Please let me know a few times that might work for you."
A bunch of boxes of supplies arrive in the main office. You are asked to send students down to get them. You ask for volunteers. After you are done choosing, a student points out you only chose boys.	"Ugh. Yes, you are absolutely right. I can't believe I did that but I did. Thanks for pointing that out. It's a reminder of how we can make mistakes that unconsciously reinforce bias. I have to be more careful that my actions match my beliefs. So glad that you all are thinking about these things and that you were willing to speak up! As a community, one of our responsibilities is to hold each other accountable and I'm not above that."
You do a robotics lesson. Because the robots are part of a commercial kit, you didn't double-check what was in the kit. As the students get to work, they realize there are missing parts. Students who have missing parts aren't able to build their own robot and must work with a partner. They loudly grouse.	"Wow. You know what I failed to do that scientists should always do? Check to see that all my materials were ready before I started working. You all can learn from my mistake. When we're doing an experiment or putting something together, our first step is to make sure we have all the materials. I should have done that, and I was wrong. I'm sorry."

Figure 1-2 **Acknowledging Impact**

students, we are reinforcing the idea that students are somehow less worthy than us. That we don't need to explain ourselves to them. When we own up to our missteps, we are showing our staunch belief in their worthiness. Additionally, when students see that we are actively learning and growing in front of them, they can really believe that we mean it when we invite them to make mistakes and learn from them in the classroom. When we talk about directly teaching students lessons about mistakes, we discuss the ways we can teach impact and intent directly to students. But that work will go a whole lot better if the students have seen it modeled for them before by us.

THE CONSEQUENCES OUR STUDENTS AND FAMILIES FACE VARY WIDELY

Of course, impact is not going to be the same for every person; equity and equality are not the same. Although it can be difficult for us to acknowledge the amount of power we have in our students' lives, it is true that for many students and their families, teachers are some of the people who wield the greatest power. And the greater the power, the greater the impact of our actions—both good and bad. This awareness matters because the more power we have, the more insulated we can be from the cost of our mistakes.

Think about a fairly regular mistake people make all the time, one that you might have even made today—you get distracted and blow through a stop sign. If a police officer pulls you over, what happens next likely has a direct connection to your skin color, gender presentation, amount of money in your bank account, previous arrest record, who else is in the car with you, age, detectable disability, immigration status, donations to particular organizations or affiliations known by stickers on your vehicle, and more. Depending on your identity, this traffic stop can range in impact from a minor interruption in your day to a life-altering event. Scroll through the news on your phone. Flip through the twenty-four-hour news channels. Notice the protests in the streets. I doubt any of us would say that although everyone makes mistakes, everyone pays for them equally. The consequences for mistakes are largely determined by how marginalized or privileged our identities are in society.

It's not just that our mistakes affect us differently because of where *we* stand in the world but also that our mistakes affect students differently because of *their* identities. This is true not just during traffic stops. The cost of a mistake—any mistake—is either enlarged or reduced by your identity and the identity of those responding or reacting to the mistake. Mistakes cost more for some and less for others—even when the mistake is exactly the same.

APOLOGIES NEED TO BE EQUITY MINDED

If equality is everyone getting the same and equity is getting what is needed, we must remember that that definition of equity applies to everything, including our own responses to mistakes we made. If I am feeling anger toward my administrator or my class when I'm entering report card grades and I grade much more harshly than usual, only to realize later that it was a mistake to not calm myself down before grading, the impact of those grades will not be the same for everyone. Certainly the student whose parents don't put much stock in grades is not nearly as affected as the student whose mom punishes for poor grades or the student whose ability to play on the soccer team is contingent on grade point average. When we own our impact, we need to see each person we harmed as an individual with individual harm done, and we cannot expect that our blanket acknowledgment or apology will do the same work for everyone.

And, since we are modeling for our students how to acknowledge impact, we have to proceed with caution on this one. Although our response should be sincere and public enough that students understand we are owning our impact, it should not come at the cost of making the most impacted student an example for others to learn from. We do not want to share information about our students that could be personal or make them feel vulnerable. We all know the extreme discomfort of being the unwanted focus of attention as a student. For some students, that experience results in real trauma that disengages them from school. One teacher I spoke with recalled stepping in to defuse an altercation in the hallway. One student responded by saying something sexually explicit to her. She completely lost her temper, in a way that she knew was wrong at the time. Later, because she knew everyone was talking about the incident, she wanted to apologize publicly to the student because she knew there was a lot of shame and a power dynamic in play. But fortunately she thought to ask the student first. He didn't want a public apology at all, so she apologized privately. We should be clear when discussing our mistakes publicly that our fumble was one that did not affect everyone equally. I might choose to pull students aside who were more likely to have paid a higher cost, but probably better still would be to also leave the door open for students who would like to speak with me about themselves or others who could have been impacted by my mistakes. "Hey, everyone. I know I messed this up," we might say. "If anyone wants to discuss this with me privately, or send me a note, please know I welcome hearing more from you. I'm going to be reflecting on this on my own, but I'd be glad to hear your thoughts." That said, there are no hard-and-fast rules about the best way to apologize without causing greater harm.

An undercurrent of all our teaching must be to show through our actions and words that although mistakes happen, the mistake-maker must never lose sight of impact.

Where We Are in the Power Hierarchy Matters

But sometimes we do lose sight of the impact. Sometimes we feel so bad about making a mistake that we can't sit with the discomfort and instead turn the responsibility over to the victim. A classic example, one that I have been a perpetrator, victim, and witness of, is when kids get unruly. The educator is trying to get something done (attendance, teach a lesson, pass something out, and so on). The educator loses their temper and yells. The students flinch. The educator says, "See what happened? You were out of control and I had no choice but to yell!"

In our calmer moments we could likely trace the mistake back to what happened even before the big blowup to smaller errors. Perhaps we didn't give the students enough direction before we got distracted. Perhaps we didn't explain how important the students' quiet was to the task at hand. Perhaps we gave no purpose to their current work. If we had done that, the chances are the students wouldn't have become unruly. So, even if we wanted to pin the mistake on the students, we would need to acknowledge we still had a certain level of ownership of the events leading up to it.

Sometimes when I make a mistake I am not ready to own up to, I ask myself to consider what happened before. What might I have done, not two minutes before but perhaps hours, days, or weeks ago that might have led to this mistake? A fifth-grade teacher shared with me her recent frustration with the families of her students. They regularly sent her little text messages, emails, and notes that were more than informational or important questions. They shared personal details about their lives that made her feel uncomfortable and asked questions late in the evening about things they could probably have figured out themselves. Worse, they got salty and made passive-aggressive remarks if she didn't respond to them. As she talked it through, at first she thought it was because this batch of families had little respect for her. But, as she started comparing notes to other colleagues in her building, she realized that perhaps, at the beginning of the year in an effort to be friendly and inviting, she had done a lot to break down healthy boundaries. "As I was complaining to a friend, I started telling the story of back-to-school night and realized that they were actually pretty quiet. It made me nervous, like I thought maybe they didn't like me. So I started reiterating how important I thought it was for them to feel like they could contact me at any time for *anything* and I would get back to them within twenty-four hours. And I didn't just mention that once. I mentioned it a lot and even said it again in my newsletter and anytime I saw them at drop-offs or pickups. And when they started to send me these notes, I responded right away because I was so concerned about not appearing cold and wanting them to like me." Her face turned red. Yes, the families were becoming overwhelming in their demands, but it hadn't come from nowhere.

MISUSING OUR POWER BY SHAMING STUDENTS

In one of my most regrettable mistakes in the classroom, one of my students, we'll call him Larry, had been identified by his parents as gifted. We didn't have a gifted and talented program in our school. Whether you agree with the concept of gifted and talented as a category, Larry's self-perception as such is important to this story. The year Larry was in my class, I taught in a collaborative model where there were two teachers with thirty two students. Roughly 40 percent of the students had individualized education programs. They had a wide range of strengths and needs. I don't remember how it started, but one of the students who received support with decoding read aloud a message to himself. One of the words on the message was *does*, but he read it as *dews*. Without missing a beat, Larry guffawed loudly and pointed at the student who misread the word. "Oh my God! You just read *does* wrong. *Does*? I mean, what are you, retarded?" he yelled.

In a flash I was screeching at Larry to get out of the class, "Meet me in the hallway! We do not call people slurs in this classroom! We especially do not humiliate people when they make mistakes!" As soon as we got into the hall I really laid into Larry. I'm sure the whole class could hear me. My teaching partner stepped out to check on us. When she saw that it was OK to jump in, she bent down to his level and said calmly, "Do you understand why Colleen is so upset right now?"

He nodded. Tears in his eyes. And all at once I saw my mistake. In my effort to protect one student from shame, I had self-righteously shamed another. I took a deep breath and my rage and protectiveness melted away. I realized I needed to try to make this right. We returned to the classroom. I first checked in on the student who had been made fun of. And then I apologized. I acknowledged that what Larry had done was wrong, and it was never going to be an OK thing to do. However, I also explained that my response was terrible, and had possibly made things worse.

One of the biggest challenges in owning one's mistakes as an educator, or as a parent, or as a caregiver, is when a student does something that is worthy of response, and our own response is outsized or just plain wrong. This is difficult because mistake owning is always hard, but also because we often teach in cultures where power dynamics and discipline philosophies are not always the healthiest for kids. We might teach in schools that very much operate under the "seen and not heard" philosophy. We might teach in schools that view one kind of student behavior and work ethic as the right one. We might teach in schools where quiet and submissive classroom management is the only one that is valued so students who need more movement and music and sound are gravely at risk of never learning in a school environment that values their person. Sometimes we risk ceding some of our power to a student who challenges us; sometimes we are at risk of losing the esteem of our colleagues. It can take some serious introspection and humility to take the step of owning a mistake publicly. And yet, we are also likely familiar with the Quaker saying, "Speak truth to power" (American Friends Service Committee 1955). We know that when our students see or hear us share stories of speaking up for them instead of complying, especially after we make a mistake that impacted them, they learn valuable lessons about the importance of both examining intent and mitigating impact. They also learn to consider the ways one can speak truth to power, with the power of doing right supporting you. This sort of move, although possibly frightening to contemplate, is the sort of modeling that can allow our students to see the possibilities for themselves speaking their own truths and the truths of others to power. Including, which we should brace for, speaking hard truths to us.

TRACING THE PATH OF OUR MISTAKES WITH TIMELINES

This is helpful reflection work to do in any aspect of our lives, but it is especially important to do when we make mistakes from a position of power. It is fairly easy for people in power to "punch down" even though we know from our schoolyard days we should always pick on someone our own size. However, how often have I heard of schools chastising children for coming to school without something that was completely outside their control (lunch, pencils, permission slip money, a good night's sleep)? How often have we seen letters from schools and school districts go viral that explain things the school is not responsible for (dress code, manners, a work ethic)? Although it is easy to feel as if schools are powerless and families and kids have all the power, for many of our students and families, this is not the case. Schools have a tremendous amount of power, both actual and symbolic. When schools shift the blame of an issue they are having with students to the students or their families, they are both evading responsibility and not owning the school's actual position of power. See Figure 1–3.

And when our choices have effects that go beyond ourselves, we owe it to the people we are responsible for to own those choices. When this reflective work is tough to do, when I really feel like there couldn't possibly be an inciting, preventable mistake I can point to, I find it helpful to sketch a quick timeline and trace back a bit until I hit a point where a different decision could have been made. See Figure 1–4 for two examples.

That teacher I mentioned earlier who blamed her students for her yelling at them? She could have paused, reflected on her actions, and, if she felt stuck, scribbled out a quick bulleted list of the events of the day or just spent some time thinking about it while preparing dinner that night. I have faith that most practitioners would start to connect the dots and see places where they could have made different choices that would have led to different outcomes. Then whether that day or someday soon, she could have said to her class, "You know what, the other day I blamed you for my yelling at you. I said you were out of control and deserved to be yelled at. But I should never have said that. I did some reflecting on that because it didn't feel right to me and it's not the kind of teacher I want to be or you deserve. Yes, you were not behaving well. But no one deserves to be yelled at. And there are things I could have done as an adult to help you to remember our class guidelines. I apologize." Knowing that there are things I could do even before I start throwing blame fingers can not only help me learn from my mistakes but also help me make this process more visible to my students.

Timelines might not be the right reflection tool for every teacher, at least not at first, but spending some time at the end of each day or week writing down thoughts about what you noticed, what made you uncomfortable, what you know you want or need to do better can make a difference when studying our own mistakes. Whether it's voice memos, short vlogs, or even a bullet journal, this act of reflecting and recording changes our practice, allowing us to avoid or remedy mistakes faster than we would without the practice of reflection.

Instead of this . . .	You might try this . . .
Taking away recess, field trips, or special events for incomplete assignments or homework	• Disconnect exercise, enrichment, and socializing from academic demands and treat them as separate items with separate guidelines. • Investigate student resources, family schedules. Consider whether the assignment is accessible to all students or whether there are ways it can be made more so.
Employing blocker programs or only using white pages to minimize student access to inappropriate or distracting aspects of the internet	• Explicitly teach students internet best practices, including what sites are appropriate for school, how everything is tracked, and legal ramifications for certain behaviors. • Actively meet with and confer with students while they are using online tools, naming and coaching into pitfalls you see.
Sending out a letter scolding families for student dress, manners, and studiousness and pointing out how these behaviors start at home	• Consider if students have access to the clothing required in the dress code and the means to purchase, launder, and prepare those clothes. • Explore ways to explicitly teach into the culture and habits your school values, knowing that families either might not be aware of them or might not prioritize them for good reason.
Creating tracking systems and awards and incentives for reading and punishments for not reading to increase student volume of reading, vocabulary growth, and academic achievement	• Study whether or not the school community is in a book desert where students have little or no access to books outside of school. • Visit the local public library to see if there are systems that might be barriers to students and their families that could be revised (documentation required for library card applications, fines, staircases at entrance, no public transportation). • Team with businesses to offer book ownership opportunities to students as well as make school library lending more accessible. • Reduce or remove imposed accountability measures, focusing instead on book clubs and conversations.

Figure 1-3 Shift from Blame to Action

Mistake: Read aloud a short text with a dramatic turn to illustrate a point. Look up and see one of the students is crying. When you investigate, you discover that the student has experienced a trauma similar to the storyline.

Timeline:

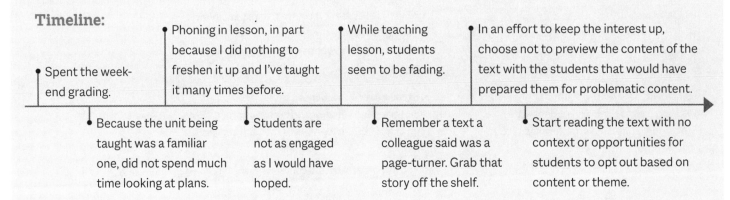

Phoning in lesson, in part because I did nothing to freshen it up and I've taught it many times before.

While teaching lesson, students seem to be fading.

In an effort to keep the interest up, choose not to preview the content of the text with the students that would have prepared them for problematic content.

Spent the weekend grading.

Because the unit being taught was a familiar one, did not spend much time looking at plans.

Students are not as engaged as I would have hoped.

Remember a text a colleague said was a page-turner. Grab that story off the shelf.

Start reading the text with no context or opportunities for students to opt out based on content or theme.

Mistake: Give students unit test where more than half fail. When you look at it closely, you realize there is an entire section of the test that asks for knowledge you haven't taught.

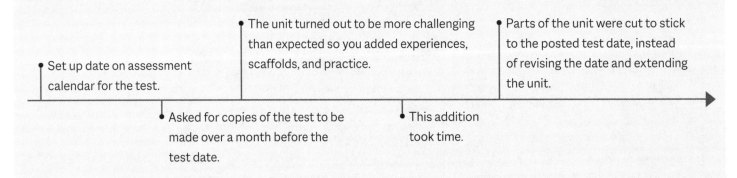

The unit turned out to be more challenging than expected so you added experiences, scaffolds, and practice.

Parts of the unit were cut to stick to the posted test date, instead of revising the date and extending the unit.

Set up date on assessment calendar for the test.

Asked for copies of the test to be made over a month before the test date.

This addition took time.

Figure 1–4 Timeline Mistake Analysis

OTHER PEOPLE'S MISTAKES

Recognizing the Desire to Judge Others

It would do us good to admit that most of us are significantly less judgmental and more accepting of our own errors. Research confirms that we are excellent at self-justification for our own mistakes (Tavris and Aronson 2015). But I think many of us also know we are not so good at showing that same level of justification and empathy toward the mistakes of others. This hypocritical life philosophy isn't only problematic because it alienates us from other people— everyone makes mistakes when I make a mistake, but *you* really messed this up when *you* make a mistake—it is also an obstacle to creating the trusting and risk-encouraging schools and classrooms students need to learn.

Our immediate emotional responses in the face of student error can have a direct effect on the learning relationship we have with the student and how their peers might feel about making mistakes in our classroom. When a student takes a clear risk while learning a new mathematical formula, we usually applaud their attempt and help them wipe the sweat off their brow, even if the mistake was one they could have managed to avoid. However, when that same student forgets to bring in their signed unit test or is unkind

15

to a classmate, those mistakes are looked at as somehow worse and worthy of silent lunch recess or being removed from class. Accepting developmental approximation will result in that student feeling as if their hard work is valued and imperfection is OK. Expecting perfection sends a clear message that behavioral mistakes have a lower threshold and higher cost. Our fixed judgments about behavior or even the students themselves means that we see behavior and morality as rigidly linked: bad behavior is an irredeemable moral failure. Even though we logically know that both learning mistakes and behavioral mistakes are actions and one can make mistakes when taking any type of action, it can be challenging to let go of the knee-jerk reaction that behavior is tidily binary.

There's a strange kind of comfort in clear and rigid definitions of *good* and *bad*. The act of categorizing allows us to disengage from situations and other people who violate what we believe is good and frees us to put our energy into something else. It allows us to believe that the world is more ordered than it truly is and convinces us of our rightness in this world order. To get past that mistaken belief, we have to admit that *good* and *bad* are really just placeholders for *perfect* and *imperfect*. The expectation of perfection, and the belief that only the perfect is good, can leave people feeling scarred and unworthy. In this broken belief system, some don't take risks because they are convinced of their pending failure, and others don't acknowledge their mistakes because they are convinced of their own perennial perfection. Many teachers carry buried shame at what we think are the secrets of our own imperfections or badness. And this belief system—a mistaken one—radiates out from us to others, communicating that a relationship with us means dwelling in a universe where you are either perfect and good or imperfect and bad, a universe with no space for learning or growth. But mistaken beliefs can be corrected, and we can move past the categories of good and bad, perfect and imperfect to create space for students to do their own messy learning and for our colleagues to be better than their worst mistakes.

Think back to the last time you saw a colleague mess up. It could be that you saw them approach a parent in a way you knew was going to escalate a situation, or you witnessed them losing their cool in front of their class. Although you likely weren't rooting against them, there was a way in which it was probably difficult to look away. To me it's like the last time I watched a professional sports team play, a baking championship, or an Olympic performance. I was just as glued to the competitors' stumbles as their triumphs.

This ability to sit back and comment on other people's performance even has a name: *armchair quarterback*. I am never as great a baker as when I am watching *The Great British Bake Off*. I see the competing bakers fail to separate the eggs on the technical challenge and I click my tongue knowingly. I am at my most expert when watching other people make mistakes.

Although it can be incredibly difficult to name mistakes *we* have made, both cognitively and emotionally, it is also true that many of us have no problem at all rattling off the mistakes, or perceived mistakes, of others. Go ahead and try this for yourself. Name a person you know well. It can be a student, an administrator, a colleague, or someone outside of school like a spouse, relative, politician, or even your favorite bagel guy. Now, name a few of their most recent mistakes. You can write them down or just tick them off across your fingers.

How did it go?

I found myself having no trouble at all thinking of lists and lists of mistakes that other people make. In some cases, I can even sort out other people's mistakes into categories. Big, medium, little. Forgivable and unforgiveable. Always makes this mistake, sometimes, rarely. Mistakes that affect me. Mistakes that I can overlook.

For the most part, I feel rather magnanimous about their mistakes. And yet, let's be honest, the fact that I will invest the time to label and sort them shows that I'm still holding on to some judgment. Our first instinct to other people's mistakes is often judgment and punitive responses when possible. When we frame the narrative of someone's mistake that way, we usually hold on to that judgment to some degree long past the time of the mistake. Shifting to reframing the narrative around other people's mistakes to empathy and understanding requires conscious effort.

In schools we can see this play out in all kinds of ways. We get cranky when our class is interrupted loudly by a service provider pulling kids at the wrong time by mistake. Or a student running to class slams into us and we immediately jump to the conclusion that they are disrespectful. Or, we go to teach a lesson that is crucial to our grade, only to discover that not a single student knows the prerequisite concepts that should have been taught the previous year. Steam feels as if it's pouring out of our ears. There are legitimate reasons for feeling this anger, of course. Many of us have stories where it is clear that somehow a student has been handed from grade to grade with very few skills. How does a sophomore show up to English class reading at a first-grade level and no one gave them the support they needed? Bad teaching does happen and when it does, we have every right to feel righteous anger on our students' behalf. The student experienced educational neglect, which is not a mistake but an intentional wrongdoing. However, it is also the case that sometimes we leap to conclusions as to whose responsibility and mistakes led to this situation, and it would be wiser to hold our rage at others' trespasses until we know the truth. Wiser still to redirect that energy into addressing the problem.

We can get so, so judgy about other people's mistakes. And sometimes that's OK, if it leads to a healthy conversation. When yet another interruption by a service provider happens, we can quietly and warmly take the person aside and suggest, "Hey, can we go over your schedule and a strategy for picking up students for your program? There's been a couple of mishaps lately, and I'm thinking it might help to refresh at this point in the year to see if anything has changed or needs adjusting." It can be healthy, too, to take a moment

I found myself having no trouble thinking of mistakes that other people make.

and acknowledge our feelings, to let ourselves get judgy at someone else's stumbles, for a moment, with the intention of using that knowledge to consider how we can avoid similar errors. For example, we could really fine-tune our assessments and instruction so that we're sure every student is ready for the expectations of the next year. Or, and maybe this is sort of ugly, but also healthy, if by taking a moment to be judgy, without sharing that judgment with anyone else who could do harm to the person being judged, it triggers a ca-tharsis of sorts, a justified chance to blow off some steam, then OK, take your moment. But try not to turn that moment into a fixed sense of who the person you're judging is. That's psychic pollution. I'm not saying it's easy. I work on it every day, with some days being more successful than others, some relationships more judgment free than others.

New Narratives for Mistake-Making

A teacher I recently spoke with, Clara, was struggling with her colleagues' fixed judgment. Money had gone missing from several classrooms—some from class trips and some from teachers' wallets. Reviewing the school's video footage showed a group of students had committed the theft together. The administration met with the teachers who had been stolen from to discuss options for the school's response. Clara said, "There were two sides. On one side were the teachers who decided that these kids were bad seeds and nothing could be done for them. They needed to lose everything, including the senior trip and walking at graduation. On the other side were the teachers who knew these kids and felt like this was normal kid behavior and that they should get a firm talking to and that was that. I was shocked. Nobody wanted to try to investigate to figure out what led these kids to act in this way or give them an opportunity to make amends. The only options were this absolute dichotomy. These kids were either all good or all bad, and there was no wiggle room and no belief they could be any other way."

At that moment of impasse, the group of teachers needed to move toward a third way, to find a new story for themselves and the students. They needed a framework for construc-tive inquiry, one that collaborated with the students who had stolen and the teachers who had been stolen from in a way that would allow for the students' positive reentry into the community. Not shaming or ostracizing. This work of restorative justice can be hard to do but it is a better narrative. It requires us to tell different stories about mistake-making, one that creates a community that recognizes mistakes as an inevitable part of being human. Restorative justice is a conversation between those who have been violated and those who have done the violation, focusing on reconciliation and rehabilitation instead of pun-ishment. Unlike common responses to crimes and misbehavior, restorative justice repairs the crime in the community. Restorative justice has become more common in schools as educators and activists recognized the link between school discipline practices and prison (commonly called "the school to prison pipeline"). The idea of restorative justice in school is that students will take an active role in problem-solving. The Centre for Justice & Reconciliation describes this process as having four corner posts:

1. inclusion of all parties

2. encountering the other side

3. making amends for the harm

4. reintegration of the parties into their communities.

One of the most important understandings about restorative justice is that the solution depends on the context. No one outside the situation can say that there needs to be one set solution because that depends entirely on the individuals involved. So although I can't say what the right third way for those students and teachers would have been, I can say that it would have been right for them to have focused on responsibility, healing, and forgiveness; and that there would have been learning for everyone involved. (For resources on restorative justice, see page 51. I'll talk more about what forgiveness can look like in the classroom in the pages that follow here.)

. . . .

Restorative justice is not yet a common story in our culture. Right now, we're recognizing a narrative failure in American culture. This narrative failure comes from an overreliance on one story, the hero's journey. Joseph Campbell, a literature professor, popularized the idea that all stories are the hero's journey, with the intention of emphasizing the universal patterns shared by every culture. Although a useful observation, Campbell insists on a reductive and damaging vision of what's possible for stories, real or invented, not to mention a troublesome idea of what make a "universal" pattern. Are we the hero, the helper, the victim who needs rescuing, or the villain? We say what we want to be; we imagine ourselves to be the hero. But are we really? Do we hold ourselves to the expectation that we alone should be able to overcome adversity? And if we're the hero, that means anyone who wrongs us, either volitionally or accidentally, is the villain. This creates a judgmental distancing where people are either serving our needs or obstacles to our success. And if we're not succeeding despite adversity, then we're the victim whose job is to wait to be rescued or, worse yet, not even part of the story. Educational narratives are fraught with heroes and villains.

    Although I believe in the potential in every human being to do great things, I know that the heroic narrative sets too many people up for failure and exclusion, especially teachers

Educational narratives are fraught with heroes and villains.

and students. It lets us pretend that systems don't need to be changed and that failure belongs only to individuals. This narrative is false. Too many teachers hide in shame, do less than they could, or burn out by doing more than they can manage. They've been gaslighted to believe any struggle in teaching is just a failure of their own intelligence, compassion, and imagination. And, again, if they can't take on that mantle, then they're the villain, the victim, or not in the story. So, when a student challenges our way of working, the student too easily becomes the villain. Because if we believe our only identity choices lie in that narrative, then we have to hold on to ways we can be the hero. The hero's journey gives us a limited vision of what's possible for us and our students. Instead of a narrative with heroes, villains, victims, and helpers, where other people's mistakes require us to take defensive postures, we need stories about community. In stories that emphasize community, we can look to examples such as Rev. Dr. Martin Luther King's vision of "beloved community," one that centers the collective community over any one individual. Community narratives acknowledge conflict as unavoidable but, instead of seeing it as a story of winners and losers, reframes the story of conflict as one of collaborative problem-solving with the goal of communication, acceptance, and inclusion (The King Center 2019). True community is the story of conflict and connection. In other words, instead of fatalistically accepting the hero's journey as the primary narrative of teaching, perhaps we can come to consider something more along the lines of Ursula Le Guin, who describes a different vision of narrative, one of connections, disconnections, and connections. "The traditional story revolves around conflict—a requirement Ursula K. Le Guin disparages as 'the gladiatorial view of fiction.' When we're taught to focus our stories on a central struggle, we seem to choose by default to base all our plots on the clash of opposing forces. We limit our vision to a single aspect of existence and overlook much of the richness and complexity of our lives, just the stuff that makes a work of fiction memorable" (Lefer 1994). Let's look at Figure 2-1 for what that might look like.

This narrative shift helps us hold on to the understanding that people are more likely to take positive risks when they are treated compassionately (Lee et al. 2004). When they are treated harshly, out of frustration or anger, they prioritize avoiding that treatment again over their own learning and growth.

Of course, moving from a heroic to community narrative requires us to dismantle our schema of how relationships should go. Everything—from a soda commercial to newspaper headlines to the latest blockbuster—tells us the story of one individual or group dominating another. Good guys, bad guys, dominance or defeat. When we find ourselves with unhelpful emotional responses to student mistakes, the easiest next step is to default to those negative emotions and imagine ourselves the hero or victim, the student, the villain. We can retrain ourselves to respond in more constructive ways.

Hero's Journey	Community Narrative
Incident: A student cheats on a class project.	
Interpretation: The student is the villain who has violated the agreed-upon moral code that the teacher, the hero, must protect. This student will receive a zero and academic probation that prevents them from participating in team sports and afterschool activities.	**Interpretation**: The teacher doesn't know the student's reason for cheating without a conversation with the student, but it is clear some sort of disconnection is at play. Whether the student is disconnected from the content, the teacher, or perhaps the larger school community, work needs to be done to find ways to help the student connect. A punitive response will likely result in more disconnection, not less, so the teacher works as connector, first investigating the source of the disconnect, and then supporting the student to connect.

Figure 2–1 Two Narratives Around Other People's Mistakes in Schools

According to Emma Seppälä (2015), the best way to do this is to follow a three-step process. First, we take a moment to settle ourselves down and recognize what we're feeling. We are entitled to feel however we want to feel, but we are responsible for controlling how we behave; we don't have to behave based on our emotions. Being able to separate the two—feelings from actions—can be difficult but our ability to emotionally regulate ourselves is an essential piece of our work as teachers. Checking in with ourselves and calming ourselves down needs to be part of our daily practice so that we avoid acting out of anger and exasperation. Second, engage in empathy. Once you have checked in with yourself and taken care of your emotional state, imagine yourself as the person (or student) in similar circumstances, considering their particular perspective. How would you feel? And third, forgive the mistake. Outwardly and generously. Let's get into the specifics of how this work can be challenging and what we can do in our classrooms to get past the challenge and onto connecting with students around mistake-making in productive, nurturing ways.

MISTAKES THAT TRIGGER RAGE AND SHAME

It is likely you have mistake triggers. Mistakes that you find more difficult to respond well to. All of us do. Although you might need to think a bit about what your triggers are, and in fact you might not even be aware of all of them, the chances are good that your students are well aware of what things set you off. In my personal life I like to call what happens to me after I am triggered my *Fish Called Wanda* response. In that old movie, the character of Otto, played by Kevin Kline, frequently gets triggered when he is called stupid. He acts completely irrationally, often to his own detriment. Now, although no one should be called stupid, the point is of course that his response always makes matters worse. When it comes to mistakes, I have my *Fish Called Wanda* responses where, despite the fact that I know better, I find myself responding in a way that I know is destructive.

For me, I am often triggered when I perceive a student's behavior is hateful to another student. I can put up with a pretty large amount of meanness to me. After all, I'm the person in power and expect students to punch up. However, when they are cruel to each other—when they pick each other's weakest or most vulnerable point and cross a line—that can be difficult to take. Their mistake could be perceived as intentional wrongdoing, but it could also be a miscalculation or a joke; *our* mistake can be in how we respond. Yes, most students know they shouldn't be saying or doing something mean, and some do it anyway. But our response to those moments should be more than righteous indignation on the victim's behalf; we need to avoid responses that shame and punish and choose ones that offer restorative justice. It can be very difficult to choose the latter because we've grown up and exist in reward-punishment systems of control. But to not do so is a mistake. So, for example, consider my reaction to the following situation. A student in my class bumped into another student. When that student snapped at him, he responded, "Why don't you go tell your mother!" Knowing her mother was in the hospital, he knew he was being mean. But he couldn't possibly have known that her mother was terminally ill or that the girl would race to the bathroom in tears. Or that I would fly off the handle in response. My choice to allow myself to be triggered in that moment, and not regulate my emotions, felt OK at the time. I saw myself as righteously protecting the girl who was wronged. But, later, when debriefing with a colleague, I realized that I missed both an opportunity to teach the boy and to be a better support for the girl.

And this is problematic.

Not because ethically and morally I should do better. Or that I made a bad situation worse. Or because it's not the image of myself as an educator that I want to put forward—although these are all true. But rather, people are less likely to learn and less likely to trust us if we respond to mistakes with anger and frustration (Haidt 2003). We know that many of us, but especially children, become afraid when they are yelled at. If we're yelling or being yelled at, we're not thinking; instead, the amygdala shuts down conscious thought so that our body can focus on survival by either fighting, fleeing, or freezing. We might think, "I've only lost my temper a few times with my students/that student," but, even if we lose our temper once, we can't know for certain what a student's past experiences have been. And so by showing a strong negative judgment to a student in response to their mistake, we let the most vulnerable children know that we are like the adults who have been cruel to them in the past. One negative reaction can undo so much of the good work we've done that we need to be extra mindful of avoiding a strong negative emotional reaction. Here's what we risk if we're not careful:

- Our student can lose trust.

- We create an atmosphere where risk-taking has negative consequences.

- Our students learn that people in power, which they will be some day, respond to less powerful people's mistakes with shame and punishment.

- We can heighten students' school-related anxiety.

By reacting to our students, our students' families, or our colleagues' mistakes with anger, we are undermining our own wishes for a better world. We want the mistake not to be repeated. And yet, we are virtually ensuring the opposite. The boy who teased the girl never really connected with me in the same way again. There's no way for me to know if he or any of the other students had a heightened sense of anxiety, but I do know there was a bit of change in our interactions after that. A little more hesitancy in joking. A little more careful politeness for a while.

We can look to Emma Seppälä's writing and use it to develop a protocol for educators when responding to student error. Although almost all of the steps are the same, the one I think we need to spend the most time with is the last, added step, which differentiates it from the business-minded protocol she espouses, to give it an educational slant. See Figure 2-2.

A Possible Protocol for Responding to Student Error

1. **Take a moment.** Notice the kind of mistake the student made. Was it a sloppy, a high-stakes, a stretch, or an aha mistake? How are you feeling right now? Hungry, tired, stressed, engaged? The time it takes to take stock of these things will simply be read as a pause by the student, if it's noticed at all. The pause can be a few seconds or perhaps even a few days, depending on the mistake, you, and your schedule. No matter how pressured you might feel to respond instantly, with very few exceptions, this moment of reflection will help you to respond in a way that will enhance learning and relationship building rather than disrupt it. For many of us, this moment might happen in the company of others, either in place or later with colleagues in the teacher lunchroom. Sympathetic colleagues can often help us to see and understand things that are difficult to see in the heat of the moment. For those of us who

continues

do not yet feel we have a culture in our school for this sort of collegial support, we can use these moments to start that work. One of the best ways to create a culture of care is to ask for help.

2. **Empathize.** Imagine what was going on for the student at the point of error. Were they distracted? Perhaps there were a lot of factors to contend with? Prior knowledge to tap? Skill sets required? Consider how you would feel if you were in the student's shoes. One note about this: although it can be helpful to try to read the student's face or body language to assess how they are feeling, often their outward expression doesn't tell the whole story. I, for one, know I have a difficult face to read and people frequently assume I am feeling something different than what I am. I find it helpful to give this empathy exercise the benefit of the doubt. If you are finding it difficult to feel empathy, it might be a signal to you. Is it possible you are feeling wronged in a way that might not be easily handled immediately? Is it possible you are feeling spent and need some time to practice self-care? For many, the hardest step in this process can be the act of empathizing. If that is true for you, you might consider actively naming that and then coaching yourself to consider an empathetic mindset by asking, "If I could feel empathy for this person, how might it sound?" And even if you cannot empathize, perhaps because you cannot agree with the student's choices, start with understanding. There is much to be gained by at least trying to understand the circumstances around the student's actions. Whether you are able to go the empathy or the understanding route, the best way to achieve this is to prioritize talking with and listening to the student. Even in our best mental simulations, we are still working from our own perspective and biases. To best empathize with and understand our students, we need regularly to have dialogues with them with those goals.

3. **Forgive.** This might feel like a weird one. Most of the time the mistakes students make do not appear to be directed to us at a personal level. Yet, if we gauge our responses, we have to admit there is an element of their mistake-making that feels a bit like an affront. Why weren't they listening? Why didn't they remember what was said? Why haven't they been practicing? Pushing ourselves to forgive the mistake and to embrace our magnanimous side is especially important when we feel at our most vulnerable. It moves us away from being overly precious with our own emotions and focuses our gaze on those we are there to serve—the students. Sometimes this can feel a bit like "Fake it till you make it." And that's OK. The important piece is that we are aware that our fallback position when dealing with student mistakes should be to move quickly to the forgive stage so that we can pick back up the important work of teaching.

4. Guide. If at all possible, give an actionable, replicable tip or suggestion that the student can use right away to right the wrong or make sure their next step going forward is on the right track. This can be tricky to make genuine and not rote. Not every mistake needs to be responded to with a lesson. But often in our role as educators, our best teaching opportunities come from mistakes. When at all possible it's ideal to consider not "the next time" a similar situation happens, but rather the bigger picture identity the student is cultivating (hardworking, kid, antiracist) or big picture goals.

Figure 2-2 A Protocol for Responding to Student Mistakes

This practice requires practice. Again and again and again. Because it's not easy but it is necessary. Each time we do this, we build trust in our relationships with students and colleagues and move away from the negative forces in ourselves and our culture that limit other people's potential. That limiting, judging energy is a mistake we don't want to make.

Forgiveness can be the most difficult step, so we'll unpack what that looks like in response to student mistakes in Figure 2-3.

Scenario	Unconstructive Response	Forgiving Response
Yesenia and Lara are neighbors and worked on their science fair project together for a month. The deadline for turning it in was Thursday so that it could be displayed for the fair on Friday when families would view them. Both thought the other was responsible for bringing it in. Neither brought it in.	On Thursday, in front of the class, "The deadline was clear. You both were responsible for bringing it in. It's not fair to other students who stayed up all night to finish it in time for the deadline for you to still get to display it with everyone else. There are consequences for your actions. You will not be displaying your project at the fair. No matter what."	On Thursday, stepping out into the hallway, "I can see you are both upset. Mistakes happen, and I don't believe that either of you meant for this to happen, but it did. We need to come up with a strategy to help you become better at communicating your own and your partner's responsibility. I also want us to put our heads together to come up with the best way to deal with tomorrow that is fair to your fellow students, but also understanding of an honest mistake."

continues

Scenario	Unconstructive Response	Forgiving Response
You have been annoyed for weeks with students' cell phones going off in the middle of class, despite the schoolwide policy of no phones in class. You ask students to make sure they are turned off or on vibrate or you will need to collect the phones that ring. All seems to be going well for a few days until you are in the midst of a very dramatic part of your lesson and a student's phone goes off.	You angrily stop teaching, leap toward the sound with your palm outstretched, "That is it! Enough. I'm taking this phone and holding on to it for the rest of the week or until your caregiver comes to see me. This is ridiculous. It's disrespectful to me and to your entire class."	You look up. Pause. "I know that whoever's phone that is likely forgot to turn it off. I need everyone who has a phone on you now to reach into your pocket or bag and make sure it is turned off. And I would like all of us who want to be able to have our phones on us to remind each other to turn our phones off."
Your beginning coding class has its first big project due. You reiterated many times that students should run through their projects several times before they volunteer to share. The time to fix any bugs is before the presentation date. On the day of the presentation, the third person to volunteer is a kid who bragged a lot about how much he knows about coding. He has a big personality and it was turned on full blast when he presented. However, his project hit a glitch when a classmate tried it during the presentation.	You roll your eyes and shake your head, "This. This is what I was talking about. I told you how important it was to test everything out before you got up here and wasted our time. Now we have less time to hear from people who actually did the work."	You step in. "It looks like there's a glitch here that the programmer didn't anticipate. That happens to the best of us. Jaden, do you feel comfortable with us trying to fix the glitch together, and maybe learning a bit about what went wrong? Or would you rather take it off the screen and fix it yourself, and we'll try to see it another time?"

Figure 2-3 What Forgiveness of Students Can Look Like

Forgiveness is not passive or about a lack of accountability but about constructive attention. By consistently responding in forgiving ways, not only are we helping the individuals making errors, but we are changing the culture of the room. Students who don't anticipate harsh criticism or displays of anger are more likely to be creative, collaborative, and, of course, risk-taking.

Combatting Cancel Culture

As a queer, disabled Latina, I have mixed feelings about the strength and vehemence of so-called cancel culture and watching it become more and more named and acceptable in our schools. For those of you unfamiliar with *cancel culture*, it is term to describe shunning, via social media, a person or group based on perceived wrongdoing. Some argue it is not real, but rather an invented consequence wrongdoers complain about. Others claim it is real and an acceptable response to intentional wrongdoing. My whole life has been spent watching many privileged people commit wrongdoing or make high-stakes mistakes where the impact is incredibly high, only to walk away virtually unscathed. I have seen many others, often sharing my own or parallel marginalized identities, make similar or often lower-stakes mistakes only to be completely destroyed and discarded, in both virtual and real life. A part of me experiences a little schadenfreude when people who are not used to unfair consequences, let alone deserved ones, experience something they name cancel culture and the discomfort package that comes with it. "See! How do you like them apples?" I find myself yelling at the screen when their story of woe shows up on my feed. But no matter how it might feel in the moment to see previously unscathed people get the same over-the-top treatment that people who have been marginalized have received for years, that doesn't make it right.

Yes, there is a time and a place that heavy consequences must be paid by people who commit serious and intentional wrongdoing that has a grave impact on others. Yes, students sometimes do cross lines that have severe consequences. I am not questioning the need to respond to them. And, yes, there are plenty of times when mistakes will and must be addressed with appropriate seriousness, especially when the impact calls for it. But how many true mistakes need to be addressed severely? Are there times when we can act with compassion and grace? We also must keep in mind our own culture and background when considering our responses. Many cultural traditions value communal values such as grace and forgiveness to practice and preserve the value of compassion. These differ from more reward and punishment–based cultures, often but not always individualistic, which value punishment and reward as a means of preserving their values. When you think of a public mistake, or perhaps even an intentional wrongdoing from your past, what was your cultural community's response? That cultural response might be the one you feel most comfortable imposing, but it's not the only option.

If you find yourself arguing with me (perhaps thinking that there's a time when a kid just runs out of chances, because that's the way the world works, and it has nothing to do with power or culture), I want you to also ask yourself for whom that statement is true. I think we all know people, students and adults, who never seem to run out of chances. Grace is always extended to them. The student who is always late to class but never marked tardy.

Forgiveness is . . . about constructive attention.

The student who can mouth off to the principal and never face consequences. The student who rarely turns in assignments and yet always manages to pass. We could explore why some are seemingly immune to consequences while others are not, but I believe we know why some receive grace all the time and some rarely.

In our own classrooms and schools, we need to consider the grace we extend and whether or not we extend it equally. If our default response to mistakes, true mistakes, is to respond with grace, and students both witness it and receive it on a regular basis, what effect might that have on our communities? Might not students be more likely to extend grace to each other? Might they not be more willing to take healthy risks when they know the adults in the building do not treat every mistake the same?

When I reflect on the times in my life when someone has extended grace to me, or I have been a witness to another extending grace, the chances that I will do the same at the next possible opportunity expand exponentially.

MARTYRS MAKE MORE MISTAKES

Every career has its hero archetype: the rags to riches banker, the angelic nurse, the therapist bartender. This is no different for teachers. The teacher savior-martyr archetype appears in an endless stream of films, television, and books—from Mr. Thackeray in *To Sir with Love* to Miss Honey in *Matilda* to Jaime Escalante in *Stand and Deliver*. We have been fed the story of the self-sacrificing teacher who works themselves to the bone for the good of their students. And through that sacrifice, only because of that sacrifice, they transform their students' lives.

Outside of that problematic archetype, momentum within the job itself can push teachers toward that identity. We are often the first ones on the scene when our students need something education related—or in many cases, not education related. We are first responders. When we rush to assist a child, whether the very young or those on the edge of adulthood, we often put our own needs aside to make sure they get what they need. As teachers, we are caretakers by the nature of our positions. Our instinct almost always is to care for our students before we care for ourselves.

This is a noble ideal.

But it is also impossible. Children will always need more, so there is no clear end to the amount of giving a teacher can do. And when teachers give teaching their all, they often end up depleted, drained of the physical and emotional energy to be the sort of skilled practitioner we'd all like to be. Let me say that another way: when educators give so much to their students that they are feeling empty, they do not have the ability to do the sort of high-level thinking and creative work, let alone have the physical stamina to be the excellent teacher their children need. The heroic martyr teacher might make for great film, but it does not make for great instruction.

This can be a hard thing to hold on to when we are not only romanticized when we act as a martyr but are also encouraged and expected to do so. Many teachers report that they are gaslighted by everyone from their administrators to their colleagues when they raise the question of addressing their own needs. They are repeatedly told how important they are and how they should prioritize their well-being, and then asked to do the exact opposite. From being told they can't leave a professional development session to go to the bathroom to being expected to use their own money to create classroom libraries to being reminded to only take thirty minutes for lunch during online pandemic learning, these "little" things can collectively destabilize a teacher to the point of burnout. Each of these things feel normal, somewhat doable, sometimes inspirational . . . in theory. Sometimes they come with bragging rights, "I haven't peed since I left my house this morning!" or "I can't remember if I even ate today" or "My family conferences went so long the custodial staff kicked us out." And administrators or peers impressed with our dedication or commiserating in good-natured ways about the lack of time for ourselves can make it hard to see just how unhealthy these practices become when they become an expected and accepted part of the way teachers work.

Teachers are told to take care of themselves, but then promptly told why they can't. "The students need to see your face," a principal told one teacher who was considering taking a day off for a doctor's appointment. "And when you aren't around, those kids don't learn. When you get back it's such a mess that you'll make yourself sicker just trying to catch them all up." More often than not educators hear that by prioritizing their own needs they are somehow harming children or doing something wrong. Many of us are already prone to putting others first, so it does not take much gaslighting to convince us that putting our own needs off for as long as possible somehow makes us better teachers.

The hero martyr teacher might make for great film, but it does not make for great instruction.

The Teacher Martyr Makes Mistakes, Avoids Risk, and Observes Less

I know this, preach this, and yet am also terrible at following my own admonishments. You may know that I have a disability. It's a congenital one whose only long-term solution is two major surgeries that the doctors want to put off for as long as possible. It's mostly manageable if I take care of myself. I need to balance between regular exercise and rest, stretches and physical therapy to stay mobile. I'll never be a sprinter, but if I take decent care of myself, I can still be fit enough to teach. My doctors and physical therapists have always been crystal clear—if I want to stay in education and be as active as I am, I need to prioritize my health.

And yet, it is so easy to fall into the habit of doing everything else that seems more important than taking care of ourselves. Day after day on social media and in the news, we hear of teachers martyring themselves for the good of their students and their profession. Those are the teachers whose social media posts we share and inspire us. So, by ignoring my own needs and focusing solely on my students, I found myself crawling out of a New York subway train, across a Brooklyn platform, and dragging myself to a bench. It was a busy work week. There was a family night and grading and an end-of-unit celebration. I was staying at school every night until at least 7:00, then getting home and not eating dinner until nearly 9:00, doing some planning and grading before I'd finally collapse in a heap only to repeat the same self-punishing routine the next day. I did this day after day for over a week. No time for healthy eating, resting, stretching, or gentle exercise. Or so I thought. It shouldn't have come as a shock when I stood up to leave the subway car at my stop that my leg suddenly protested with agonizing pain and an inability to hold my weight. I had no choice but to crawl off. Some kind New Yorkers who saw me crawling helped me find a bench and stayed with me until the school secretary could come pick me up. I don't know how or when I got to the emergency room, but I do remember my principal standing over me, after he was assured I would be OK, his finger pointed in my face, saying, "You can't do this. It's not good for you. And it's not helping anyone."

You probably know all this. You have probably either lectured someone else or been lectured on how important it is to take care of yourself. Maybe you even have your own version of my subway crawling story. Perhaps for you it was pneumonia, bronchitis, or dizzy spells so bad you were hospitalized. You promised yourself you would never let it get that bad again because you saw how bad it was for everyone. But you might not have been considering how not prioritizing self-care affects the topic we've been considering throughout this book: mistakes.

When we are depleted, we are so much more likely to make mistakes we regret. These mistakes might just be the sloppy ones like leaving the cap off our beloved whiteboard purple marker or forgetting our keys in the teacher's lounge. But they can also be very high-stakes mistakes—ones that can dramatically affect children's lives. We might not have the capacity to write all of the letters of recommendations our students request. We might not carefully read the accommodations on a student's individualized education program and miss key provisions. As you sit there reading this paragraph, you might be thinking about mistakes you have made recently, or maybe ones you made a long time ago that still haunt you. Before you begin to flagellate yourself for that error that just bubbled up again, is it possible that when you made that mistake, you hadn't been your best self in terms of self-care? That you might have been tired, hungry, stressed, overwhelmed, or all of the above before you made that regrettable error?

When I look back at the mistakes I made in my own classroom or with teachers in theirs, I have to admit most of them wouldn't have happened if I had taken care of my physical, mental, and emotional state a bit more. Use the chart in Figure 3–1 to help think about your own examples.

I know that I can never hear too much about how the best defense against mistakes is a good offense. If I want to be the best educator (parent, friend, spouse, citizen) I can be, I need to take care of myself first. All other tacks and strategies will be useless without those things. I know you know this. And, if you spend any time on social media at all, you have no doubt seen the countless memes and articles extolling you to focus on self-care. If you are at all like me, you swing from rolling your eyes at people's self-centeredness to working so hard you hit a point if you don't do something (bubble bath, sip of tea, just *one* night of eight hours of sleep) you feel you will implode. That said, we are human and our souls and bodies need to be fed. We need time to laugh with loved ones, fill our minds with rich ideas and art, yes, and even time to rest and recuperate. Even lying on the couch losing ourselves in a great binge-watch can be soul-feeding self-care. Pleasure is more than a treat. As the legendary performance artist Penny Arcade says, "Pleasure is a radical value" (2016). It is a value that goes a long way toward helping us to lead meaningful and joyful lives. If we do not do the work of prioritizing our own mental and physical health outside the classroom, there might be a time where we start to look for affirmation, connectedness, and care from the students in our own classrooms. As Jaleel Howard, Tanya Milner-McCall, and Tyrone Howard (2020) wrote in their book *No More Teaching Without Positive Relationships* (full disclosure, I coedited this book with Nell Duke), "Teachers need to share themselves with students but have their emotional needs met elsewhere." We should not expect our kids to make us feel good about ourselves. If educators are spending all day with students and then every waking moment preparing to work with them again, there is no way we can prioritize our other adult relationships. And that need for connection may unconsciously

Mistake	Cause
Snapped at a kid during read-aloud who kept calling out, even though I was aware the student was a social processor and would have benefited from a discussion about other ways to process socially without being disruptive.	Tired. Stayed up late the previous night and was using all my energy on my performance of the read-aloud.
Right before the vacation, the administration asked teachers to put together packets of materials for students to do over the vacation. Frazzled, overwhelmed with last-minute responsibilities and multitasking before the break, you do not speak up to the administration about the pressure, nor do you take time to collaborate with a colleague. The packet is thrown together in front of the copier. It ends up containing way too many pages and a lot of material that was not yet covered in class. The most vulnerable students in the class return from vacation upset because they couldn't finish it and now think they don't really understand the content.	Multitasking to try to meet conflicting demands ends up with thoughtless assignments that make students feel overwhelmed and unintelligent.
Complained to a colleague in the hallway about a "struggler who is getting on my last nerve" rather than reflecting on possible instructional obstacles that are keeping the student from growing, only to realize that student overheard.	Vented frustrations as a way to relieve some of the stress felt from not being able to help the student grow.
Showed video for lesson based on a friend's recommendation it would be perfect for the class. However, the video featured a range of gender stereotypes and students were clearly upset by it.	Since the video was recommended by a friend, assumed it would be fine. On reflection, realized the friend did not even consider the audience or appropriateness, only the content. And because of being overstretched, did not either consider the lens the recommender might have used or take the time to preview the video.

Figure 3–1 **How Lack of Self-Care Leads to Teaching Mistakes**

lead us to seek affirmation from our students. Even if it's just feeling good whenever we go above and beyond. Although it might feel right or somewhat saintly to give everything we've got to our students, in the end if we do not care for ourselves outside of the classroom or are not bringing our best selves to the classroom, we might instead feel bitter and taken for granted. Or, even in some cases, we might become emotionally needy around students, seeking their approval, comfort, and affirmation, which sets up an unhealthy dynamic where kids are unknowingly trying to fulfill an adult's emotional needs and also developing an unhealthy sense of what a healthy teacher–student relationship should look like.

Although it is completely understandable to realize after the fact that the likely cause of an error was that we were not taking care of ourselves the way we should, it is less understandable and yet still very common to then not try to prevent another error by taking steps to put ourselves first. It feels strange. It feels selfish. Even our own mentors and teachers were probably models of martyrdom, and although they very likely encouraged us to take care of ourselves, they probably rarely if ever modeled it. The script everyone shows us to follow is teacher martyr.

Yet, we know in our marrow that our last regrettable mistake was very likely made because of our lack of self-care. The thing is, not prioritizing ourselves doesn't just make us vulnerable to regrettable mistakes. When we are depleted, we are also much more likely to not take the risks we need to take to make the good mistakes.

Think about it. Think about your limited energy and the level and depth of energy it takes to try something new, be creative, or take a pedagogical risk. When you do not prioritize your own health, rest, and happiness, you are less likely to have the energy to take the sorts of risks that lead to our aha moments or stretch mistakes. When you spend hours reading through summative assessments without a break, racing against the clock to get them all marked in time, you are significantly less likely to decide now is the time to try some of the latest ideas around high-quality and growth mindset–based feedback. That sort of work requires energy to take a risk as well as time to fix any trouble spots. So instead, you might do a quick online search for "great feedback for students" and click on the link that offers "100 positive phrases to use when giving student feedback." (See Figure 3–2 for other options.)

Contrary to popular belief, stretching past our comfort zones for most of us requires a calm, rested, focused self. Very few of us are tempted to push ourselves and our thinking and to challenge our most dearly held beliefs when we are feeling bad emotionally and physically. Those stretch mistakes that we encourage our kids to make require a basic foundation of self-care to be practiced.

We are also significantly less likely to be able to catch and marvel at the unexpected treasures that come up when we make aha mistakes. You might show your students a map, realize that somehow when you were prepping for the lesson last night the image on the

Instead of this...	You might try this...	So you can take a creative risk like this...
Rushing into the school building first thing in the morning and immediately racing to complete tasks that need to get done before the students arrive, creating an unhealthy sense of urgency that sets the tone for the day	Create a routine of making a cup of tea, reading a poem, visiting with a friend, or something else you truly enjoy before you begin your tasks; if you worry about time, set an alarm for when you need to stop	Drop morning work or do nows when students arrive and experiment with giving students their own version of a soft start to the day
Engaging in complaint text threads and venting in the teacher's lounge about the latest administrative or district-level demands, leaving you feeling frustrated and drained	Connect with like-minded colleagues to create a support group, designed to allow space for venting, but also to brainstorm problem-solving strategies	Present collaborative solutions to administration and district leaders when the need arises
Working through lunch, and either forgetting to eat or eating while working, so that you move into the afternoon feeling unnourished and spent	Hold a set amount of time, even if it can't be the full lunch period every day but perhaps several reserved minutes each lunch period or one full lunch per week, when you eat nourishing foods and either socialize or take some quiet time to reenergize	Experiment with more active and innovative instruction in the afternoon, after you have had your dedicated lunch times; things like project-based learning, inquiry work and student-led seminars can be tried on days you have more energy

Figure 3-2 **Self-Care and Creative Risk-Taking at School**

slide got stretched and shifted, making Africa larger on the screen. If you were rested and relaxed, you would have used that moment to talk about the differences between the more accurate Gall-Peters projection and the long used and not as accurate Mercator projection. This likely would have led to a whole discussion about colonialism and perspective and how the people with the most power preferred to show their lands as bigger than they were and more centered, even if those projections were less accurate. And how, as people are getting more and more access to information, it is getting harder and harder to put forward such slanted views without criticism. Who knows where the entire map discussion could go? But, because you need to finish this lesson right away, and you're tired and a bit embarrassed, you don't do that. You fumble a bit. Apologize for the mistake on the slide and then keep going. Teachable moment lost.

Setting Healthy Boundaries

If we acknowledge we've been influenced by the legend of the martyr teacher, then a logical next step is to look at the ways that our own actions in self-care can be an influence on our students' lives. There are countless mental, physical, and emotional ways to practice self-care. But all of them require us to begin from a place of healthy boundary setting. We cannot make time for so much as a deep breath or a cup of tea if we have no clear delineation between our own time and space and our students' and schools' demands.

At first glance it can feel rogue and selfish to contemplate what our particular boundaries are. But when we discuss our boundaries openly, and in healthy ways, we are not only setting them more firmly and giving ourselves public permission to take care of ourselves, we are also modeling for our students the ways healthy boundaries can and should be set. If we can set boundaries, they can too. Here are some examples of boundaries we might share with students along with the connections to healthy risk-taking and learning practices. As you read through them, consider if any feel like something you could say or, if not, what about that statement doesn't feel like something you would say:

- "I won't be able to meet with you during my prep period. That's the time I have my second cup of coffee, sit for a minute, and do a little professional reading before I work on my planning and other schoolwork I need to get done. If I don't do that then I am not as strong a teacher the rest of the day because I haven't gotten a chance to take a break or get ideas. I would love to meet with you during class time."

- "Thank you so much for inviting me to the school basketball game! You know how much I love going to the games when I can. But this Friday I have plans with my family to order pizza and watch movies. I haven't spent a Friday with them in a while and my family and I feel better when I do."

- "I know some of you were hoping I would have your exam results back to you by today, but last night as I was sitting down to grade, I started to feel my head nod and I realized I was far too exhausted. I knew that for one thing I wouldn't be able to give the processes you tried as much feedback as you deserved. And I knew that if I tried to push through anyway, I wouldn't get enough sleep and wouldn't be a very good teacher to you."

It is difficult to give a blanket statement about what constitutes a healthy boundary for each person. There are professional considerations and community norms to keep in mind as a starting point. But it is also true that what feels like a healthy boundary to one person can feel stifling and disconnecting to another. I am the type of person who does not answer emails after a certain time of night. I also rarely give out my cell phone number but freely give out an email address that is dedicated to correspondence with students. One of my colleagues does zero work during the weekend. Another never gives up their lunch hour. With each of these boundaries also comes a package of areas where there is a certain level of accessibility. If I choose to not work during my lunch hour nor stay late after school, it might mean that I am all in during the school day. For others it might mean they are more likely to arrive early in the morning or bring work home.

Often when we don't have time to take care of ourselves, it is because our boundaries are not healthy, clear, and firm. When we share our boundaries with our students and their families, we might consider the language we use. We don't necessarily need to say, "I have firm boundaries so don't try to cross them!" but rather, "Family time is important to me so I don't respond to emails after 6:00" or "I'm a better teacher when I have quiet time so I have a no students during lunch hour policy."

Self-Care Habits That Give Students Our Best Self

We all know self-care is important for many reasons. For example, self-care helps us to ensure we are at our most optimal health without health care interventions, according to the World Health Organization. If health for health's sake isn't enough, studies tell us that health and happiness are connected. The happier you are, the better your heart rate and blood pressure and less of the stress hormone cortisol you have in your body (which can lead to diabetes and hypertension) (Steptoe, Wardle, and Marmot 2005). Even in professions outside of teaching, studies have shown the power of self-care. In a journal for social workers, *Social Work Today*, Karen Fliny Stipp and Kyle Miller (2016) write, "Self-care is not a luxury ancillary to our professional assignments but a professional activity that makes being present and empathic a possibility. Ongoing self-care boosts our capacity to build healing relationships time and again with clients who live in trauma's wake." Many of us can read that quote and replace the term *clients* with *students and their families* and know that when we are well taken care of, we are able to better respond to students who have experienced or are currently experiencing trauma.

But few, if any of us, have spent time calculating the cost in terms of mistakes. Both being more likely to make bad ones and less likely to have the ability to reap the rewards from good ones.

To prevent mistakes, there are some things we just need to acknowledge from the start.

1. Tired and hungry people make more mistakes.

2. Multitasking people make more mistakes.

3. Unregulated emotions can lead to mistakes.

4. Making assumptions (that something is a fact, our judgment of a person or a situation) leads to more mistakes.

There are of course things missing from this list. Often more than one thing is in play. But chances are, if you think of the last mistake you made, you can recall that at least one thing on the list was present. I am going to suggest you look at your current teaching life and realities. Sleeping enough, getting enough nutritious food, pruning our to-do lists so that we feel less pressure to multitask, proactively exploring and tending to our myriad emotions, and moving through the world with the knowledge that what we think we know is true could very well not be will go a long way toward preventing the most common mistakes.

To say this more strongly, despite the repeated proclamation of how teachers have the best job in the world and staunch belief that we get paid back 100-fold in knowing we've helped others, teachers need to take care of ourselves first and foremost. When considering the martyr teacher narrative, the consequences are often left out. Mr. Thackeray gave up his dream job of being an engineer. Miss Honey gave up her inheritance. So seriously, and I say this as much for myself as for anyone reading this book, if you incorporate nothing else, please consider this—take care of yourself. When you do, you will be doing right by not only yourself and those closest to you but also, importantly, your students.

ARE YOU MEETING YOUR OWN BASIC NEEDS?

To minimize the chances of mistake-making, begin with basic survival needs. I know that sounds obvious. And yet, the number of times I have heard an educator admit to not sleeping, eating, or peeing is too high to count. Sometimes it can be difficult to even know what good self-care looks like when we are all operating in a state of emergency all the time. It can be helpful to reflect on foundational self-care (see Figure 3–3) to gage what we're doing well and what we need to work on, both individually and within our school community.

One thing I realized as I embarked on the journey that began this book a few years ago was that I rarely, if ever, thought too much about my best learning self. The one that is least likely to make harmful mistakes and the most likely to make the ideal mistakes. I wonder if you have thought about that before. If not, I am going to ask you to consider the self-care assessment for a few minutes. How did you do? Are there areas you were mildly aware could be a problem and now know could be adversely affecting your ability to teach well?

Self-Care Self-Assessment

Read through the following items. Mark them on a scale from 1–5 with 1 being never and 5 being always.

_____I sleep 7–8 hours a night.

_____I eat breakfast, lunch, and dinner.

_____My food choices are healthy.

_____I spend time alone meditating, praying, practicing mindfulness, or just being quiet.

_____I take time to socialize with friends or family.

_____I have hobbies, sports, or artistic endeavors I engage in regularly.

_____I spend time or money on grooming care such as haircuts, manicures, bubble baths.

_____I take time to regularly work out, take walks, play sports, or engage in another physical activity.

_____I read for pleasure.

_____I engage in professional development of my choosing that energizes me.

_____I enjoy entertainment such as watching movies, television, going to the theatre, attending concerts, or playing video games.

_____I make and keep regular appointments with my general practitioner, dentist, eye doctor, and any health specialists.

_____I actively work to maintain and support my mental health through such things as attending therapy, belonging to support groups, or participating in drug, alcohol, or other addiction support services.

Once you have finished the survey, look for all the areas where you scored a 1 or 2. These are area you likely need to prioritize when making time for self-care.

Figure 3-3 Self-Care Self-Assessment

Imagine what you would be like if you did most or even all of the things on the list. Picture yourself in that well-cared-for state and how you would have dealt with one of the mistakes you find most regrettable. You might even want to take a few moments to write down two versions of the situation where the mistake was made, whether in a journal or on a scrap of paper. In the first, consider how it happened, including whatever level of self-care and health you were working with at the time. Try to tease out the origin of the error.

And if you can't quite recall, use what you know about your typical pattern of behavior to suppose the most likely origin. Then, try rewriting the situation again, but this time, with a reimagined, well-cared-for you. How would you deal with that same scenario?

For example, I now have the habit of being metacognitive about my errors all the time (occupational hazard of writing a book about mistakes). But before that was a habit, I could look back at mistakes I made a decade ago and create a pretty reliable theory as to the likely origin of the error, in part because I know that most of the time in my day-to-day life I do not get enough sleep nor time to socialize. Even if I don't recall *exactly* what happened that led to me bungling the presentation to the district coaches, it's a pretty safe bet that one of those two things had something to do with it. If you take the time to reflect or journal about your errors, and in particular focusing on any possible role self-care might have played, you might find yourself feeling the way I did the first time I considered it. I was raised to self-sacrifice. There was nothing more noble to do. And yet, it is in that act of self-sacrifice that I must admit I am most likely to miss the greatest opportunities for growth as well as being most at risk for causing harm.

There's a Reason We're All So Tired

When we look at our endless list of things to do, something has to give. For many of us, one of the first things to go to the bottom of the list is sleep. And yet it should be one of the things we work hardest to protect.

We know that when our body sleeps, our cells heal and grow, our muscles strengthen. Perhaps of most interest to an educator who is trying to make few high-stakes mistakes and open themselves up to more good mistakes, according to the National Sleep Foundation, "One of the vital roles of sleep is to help solidify and consolidate memories. As we go about our day our brains take in an incredible amount of information. Rather than being directly logged and recorded, however, these facts first need to be processed and stored; and many of these steps happen while we sleep. Overnight, bits and pieces of information are transferred from more tentative, short-term memory to stronger, long-term memory— a process called 'consolidation.'" When I think of the bad mistakes educators have shared with me, as well as my own mistakes, I become acutely aware of how many of them are likely the result of being tired. And when I think about the time I paused, didn't take that extra risk or reflect on a mistake I just made that could have led to a new discovery, I also have to admit it was likely fatigue that caused me to miss that opportunity. Sleep is one of the most powerful and least cost-prohibitive forms of self-care that we can and should indulge in if we are serious about revolutionizing the role of mistakes in our practice.

I say this knowing what a hypocrite I am because I am writing this sentence after midnight on a Saturday night, knowing full well my children will be getting up with the sun and every second I spend on this keyboard is another second less sleep I will get. But I also write this owning that sleep is one of the hardest things for many of us to prioritize. We only have so many hours in the day and for many of us one of the few quiet times we have to sit and think is either late at night or early in the morning. And when we're not pushing ourselves to stay up late or wake up early, insomnia can become a problem. All professions can impact sleep. I hear a few common themes when I ask educators about what gets in the way of their sleeping. See if any of these sound familiar (Figure 3–4).

If you do this . . .	Then you might try this . . .
Stay up late planning, prepping, or grading on Sunday night so that you're "all ready for the week"	• Set aside a little time to work on a task each day—20–30 minutes instead of saving most of the work for Sunday. • Set a timer for work on Sunday. Anything that doesn't get done by that time must be put off until Monday. It helps cut down on procrastination as well as supports prioritizing.
Scroll through your phone to look at social media and catch up with friends instead of sleeping	• Create a weekly or monthly time dedicated to socializing. • Move your phone charger into another room and buy an alarm clock.
Have trouble sleeping because you are worrying about certain kids or all the work you need to do	• Put a notebook or worry box by your bed. Jot down your worries and make time to think about them in the morning. • Avoid doing work or talking about school in your bedroom. Reserve the bedroom for sleep and other adult activities.
Are wired and unable to fall asleep because you feel wide awake	• Avoid drinking caffeinated beverages after school. • Take a walk or talk to a friend about issues that are troubling you or find another way to wind down a few hours before your regularly scheduled bedtime.

Figure 3-4 **Getting Better Sleep**

We need to regularly talk to our students about self-care and model it for them. How many of us have been told to wear our love of learning on our sleeves? To hang the titles of the books we're reading on classroom doors, share our favorite algorithms, talk about the space lecture we went to at the planetarium last weekend? We are encouraged to do this because we know that students watch us closely. They learn more from our day-to-day actions about what it means to be a learner than our perfectly crafted lessons. We need to add visibly modeling self-care to our regular practice. Instead of saying, "Your papers need to be in by Friday so I have time to grade them all," you might say, "It's important for me to have some time on the weekend to spend time with my friends and unwind a bit. I have set up the deadline for Friday so that I can break your papers into groups and space them out equally across the next week so that I can balance reading them and giving you well-deserved feedback and maintaining my downtime." Or you might talk openly about the stress you feel in the room—perhaps because of testing or a very busy schedule—saying something like, "You know what, I have been noticing I've been so busy I haven't been eating that well recently and have skipped my regular workouts. I think I've been a little more impatient with you than usual because of it. I thought it was because of all that's going on. And I'm sure that's part of it. But it's also true that I'm not doing anything to help myself relieve the stress." You might consider unpacking guidelines you've always given, not as a rule to follow or because students "need to learn responsibility" but rather because it is a way for you to take care of yourself and be more present for them. For example, when you give students hours they can call or email or come to class for help with work, tuck in that having those set hours allows you to be fully present when you're there, and fully off duty when you're not.

We need to advocate for services and opportunities for them so that they are both cared for and learn how to take care of themselves. Although we are working on helping to provide the services and skills students and their families need, hopefully we also take time to reflect. Most of our students, just like most of us, need support with care and self-care. This is true regardless of the reputation of the community they are in. Whether the community is known for wearing exercise gear to drop-off and growing a garden for the cafeteria salad bar or known for kids making their own way to school and packing their own lunches, or something else altogether, it would be foolish to assume that any community, regardless of the caregivers' strengths and experiences, contains only experts at balancing self-care with other responsibilities. I worked as a staff developer for several years in a school populated with students from families who seemed very much tuned in to the latest research, trends, and suggestions for ways to best support student learning. Yet, when the teachers and I began to discuss self-care, we realized that making space for downtime or free play in a child's day was not something all of the families prioritized. We also realized that more students than we cared to admit were not getting enough sleep. When teachers surveyed families and students about their self-care habits (a similar survey to the one you tried earlier), they were not surprised to discover that many of the students who had a hard time focusing in class, had quick tempers, or had difficulty retaining information also had disrupted sleep, little free time, or inconsistent meal schedules. It became clear to these teachers that simply telling the students about healthy habits wasn't enough. It's important to note that healthy models of self-care are not more prevalent in households from certain neighborhoods, cultures, or socioeconomic classes than others. For many students, the adults in their lives are stretched too thin for many different reasons, and if they do engage in self-care, it might not be as visible or as discussed as would be helpful for learning purposes. The teachers who did the surveys were more committed to the need to transparently model how being a lifelong learner includes not only being an avid reader and hard worker and cultivating curiosity about the world, but also having a healthy balance of self-care that made it possible for them to take more intellectual risks.

It can be difficult to know what students' self-care or caregiver care looks like. It is tempting to rely on assumptions, stereotypes, and overheard conversations, but you might decide to give a survey similar to the one above, tailored to the information and the language that would be accessible to your students and their families. For younger students you might create a survey that students fill out with their families. For older students you might create two: one for the students and one for the caregivers. As you look over the results, consider what new insights you garner from your students. Many of us will find ourselves contemplating good days and tough days and developing a much more knowledgeable and likely compassionate response to our students' mistakes based on what we now know.

I, perhaps like you, was raised by a family who touted the importance of self-sacrifice, taught by many teachers who were honored for it, and embraced a certain nobility and pride that came from my own lack of self-care. It is a hard habit to break, especially when it feels so honorable.

Yet, when I look at students, see them pushing past exhaustion, hear them talking about the number of energy drinks they are drinking to get their homework done, see them cramming food into their mouth while literally running to class, I know that I would never tell them those were OK choices. Instead, I might first ask if a student is getting enough sleep if I notice their work is riddled with mistakes. Your colleague might keep a box of granola bars and a bowl of fruit for kids who are hungry. You choose not to make kids carry embarrassing bathroom passes to shame them for using the toilets. Knowing that we want students to prioritize themselves so that they can do what they most want and need to do, we also need to own that we must prioritize ourselves for that to truly happen.

We need to regularly talk to our students about self-care and model it for them.

COMMON COGNITIVE ERROR

Fear Makes Us Vulnerable to Mistakes

How Fear Negatively Impacts Decision-Making

Throughout human history, people have often lived in fear. Fed by the uncertainty of war, scarcity, or plague, fear rallies humans together in negative action. Although the fear-driven mistakes of our ancestors seem so obviously avoidable to us now, when you feel fear, it can be hard to remember your own capacity to respond to fear with a sense of inquiry, logic, and constructive action.

Fear is arguably the strongest of our negative emotions and the one that probably leads to the most mistakes, as well as lost good mistake opportunities. Think about it. When you are afraid you are more likely to:

- avoid
- lash out

- make rash decisions

- freeze

- be defensive.

Today's classrooms might feel a million times more evolved and rational than the days where people feared that handwashing would make you sick, yet we are susceptible to the same destructive momentum of fear. We live in a strange culture of fear right now. Globally, nationally, locally, and in our very own classrooms. Active shooter drills and lessons on climate change are coupled with the expectation that all students score high enough on multiple measures to ensure they will be able to compete in a world with shrinking opportunities. I'm finishing this book during the COVID-19 pandemic, where we have watched (or been a part of) people panic buying and hoarding toilet paper, bread, baby formula, and hand sanitizer, leaving nothing on the shelves for people who truly need those items. We've watched people deny there is anything serious going on and those who are lashing out at anyone they deem a threat.

Personal fears can accumulate into increasing levels of constant anxiety that lead to more mistake-making. These fears can play out in our teaching in some of the following ways:

- deciding you aren't good at math or writing and so relegating that teaching to a program rather than having the confidence to develop your own knowledge and decision-making

- deciding not to collaborate with a colleague for fear of being judged ✄

- deciding not to reach out to a student's family because you're afraid of how they'll react

- deciding not to deviate from the given curriculum because you're afraid that you'll get in trouble.

Those fear-led actions or inactions lead to unforced errors, to steal a phrase from baseball. When we let fear make our decisions, it is much more likely we'll choose the easiest, most familiar way of expressing our emotions. Of course, I am not suggesting that we get the choice of whether or not to feel fear and I'm definitely not saying that we should suppress our fear or any negative emotion. But instead, we need to be aware of our fear so that fear does not control our teaching.

The amygdala is the part of the brain that deals with fear. It also pauses other parts of our brains that deal with conscious thoughts so that we can just focus on the threat at

We need to be aware of our fear so that fear does not control our teaching.

hand. Generally speaking, the most common responses to fear are flight, fight, or freeze. We either run, lash out, or don't do anything.

Looking at that package of activities that happen in our brains, it shouldn't be a surprise that if our brains are hitting the pause button on our conscious thought, we might be more vulnerable to making bad mistakes or find it almost impossible to gather insights from the good mistakes.

What's great about fear is that it can help keep us out of harm's way. It also has an incredible grounding capacity when we're feeling other big feelings, like stress or sadness. If we are feeling overwhelmed by the state of the world, research shows we can shift that perspective by watching a good horror movie to get a good scare on (Clasen 2017). Not only will the fear shut off our conscious minds for a bit, but it often has the nice effect of giving us perspective. How bad can that contentious feedback session be with our principal? At least I'm not running from an axe-wielding fiend!

Because fear overrides our conscious thought, most of us don't spend much time analyzing our fears when we are in them. However, we can prepare ourselves for fear. How are you feeling right now? Take a few seconds right now to stop and check your heart rate, your breathing, if your palms or sweaty or your mouth dry. Unless you are creeped out for some reason while reading, the chances are good you're feeling very close to neutral and very unlikely to feel afraid. Now, the next time you feel fear, even a little silly one like seeing a strange shadow behind the shower curtain that makes you jump a bit before you realize it's just the socks you left hanging to dry, try to take a quick note on your bodily sensations so that you can start to train your conscious mind to monitor for fear. Increasing awareness allows you to become more adept at stepping into the fear with conscious thought instead of letting it carrying you to thoughtless action.

Rehearsing for fear reminds me a bit of growing up in southern California. When I was young, one of the first lessons I learned at the beach was to respect the ocean. The waves can be gentle but many are powerful enough to knock you over and draw you into the water. It's hard to know until the wave actually hits you what the strength might be. So, a wise body surfer knows to bend your knees and brace for every wave. That way, if the wave is big you have much less of a chance of getting knocked over. If the wave is small, no problem. If the wave is really big, and you do get knocked over, you are less likely to get hurt because you were braced for impact.

Reflecting on our fear when we are calm, like right now as you read this book, helps us to have our knees braced for when real fear hits us. We can't always tell when or if fear is coming, but bracing for it makes it much more likely we can identify it and recover quickly. It also helps us to see places of vulnerability for mistakes that we can begin to be aware of and prepare for.

Fear as Insight Giver

When we take the time to reflect on our fears, and our common reactions to those fears, we can learn more about what we value and what doesn't seem quite as important to us. When we see what other people fear, it can also give us insights into others.

I first learned this when I was an adolescent. I had, and still have, dramatically awful knees. As in, they regularly dislocate and then the patella can sometimes get stuck on another part of my leg and need to be relocated. It is a very painful and disorienting process. When I was younger, I was still working out what my body was OK with me doing or not doing. Jumping, running, dancing were all once favorite activities that my growing body changed how or if I could engage in them. And every time I dislocated my knee, as I lay on the ground in agony, waiting for someone to help me relocate my kneecap, my father would yell at me. After a particularly embarrassing situation during a game of leapfrog at a church picnic, I asked my mom why my dad yelled at me when I got hurt. She responded, "He's afraid. But he's not good at talking about how he feels so he yells to let the fear out." Now, although that didn't excuse his choice of coping skills, it did give me some insight into my father. He didn't like feeling helpless at protecting his children. He didn't like seeing me in pain. He was conflicted about giving me freedom to explore what my body could do while also keeping me safe.

When we study our own and our students' fears, not only are we better equipped at dealing with them but we are also gaining valuable insights into how that person works. Read the questions in Figure 4-1 to rank which fears feel most worrisome to you.

Of course there are many other ways common educator fears could be categorized. However, the chances are good that even if your categories are different, you recognize something in this list that you have experienced fear around. For some of us certain fears can be more at the forefront than others. By thinking more about what you can do to mitigate that category of fear, what strategies you can take to avoid the worst-case scenario that causes you to act, not think, we can prepare ourselves.

I am certainly not suggesting that we can mitigate or end all mistake-making by being conscious of our fears, but I do believe that when we move into a situation in which we know we are more likely to be set off, we can bend our knees and brace. If you find yourself the most likely to make mistakes when your career fears are involved, or when your administrator is coming for an observation, you will know that fear is likely to be in play. You can work to reduce, as much as possible, the chance of mistake-making, as well as simply acknowledge to yourself or a colleague that this career derailment is something you're fearful of.

- *Educational*—Will this student (or students) make the academic progress they need to make? Usually we have worries about students, but they can transform into fear when the difficulties do not abate or worsen or if the stakes are raised.

- *Emotional*—Will this student be OK emotionally? Or will their emotions disrupt their own or others' school experience? This fear was usually spoken of by teachers when they talked about sleepless nights. This fear stems from a child's emotional health. Teachers are sometimes afraid of anticipated students' and their families' emotional responses to various situations. We can also find ourselves afraid of the emotions and their actions when faced with them.

- *Physical*—Will my students and I be physically safe today? Although this fear has always been around, I feel that it has become more and more present in educators' day-to-day life. We are always afraid for students' physical safety, whether on the playground or in a fight in the yard. Additionally, we are now inundated with regular drills around active shooters and other physical threats. Many teachers have reported they regularly feel pings of fear in the school day and often consider ways to barricade class-room doors or what classroom items can be used as weapons in the event of a violent attack. Many a teacher reported fear about either giving or contracting the possibly lethal COVID-19.

- *Relational*—Do I have healthy relationships with my students and colleagues? We know relationships are the bedrock upon which our classrooms are built. Relationships with students, families, colleagues, and administrators can make or break academic success. Some of us get fearful when we get into conflicts that threaten these relation-ships. Some of us feel fearful within the relationships themselves. One of the most con-sistently top-ranked fears according to psychologists is the fear of being alone. When relationships don't work well, that fear can come raging to the fore.

- *Career*—If I don't do _____, is my career trajectory, or even my very job at risk? Although teaching had traditionally been considered a safe career, with the increased pressure placed on teachers based on performance, testing, and other outside factors, more and more teachers find themselves afraid for the direction of their careers. Some-times that fear can propel teachers to make decisions that go against what they believe is right for their students.

Figure 4-1 **Common Teacher Fears**

Understanding Fear at the Cultural Level

We humans have a poor track record of modulating our fear. One of my favorite books on the subject, *The Science of Fear* by Daniel Gardner (2008), goes into depth about all the ways fear changes the decisions we make. He points out how wars are won and lost, inventions created, cultures shifted through the power of fear. He also points out that humans are very bad at knowing what is worth fearing and not fearing the things we should. This is something I spend a lot of time thinking about. For example, do you remember having a lot more outside free time when you were a child? Unsupervised and unorganized? Many adults who were born in the last century do, but that freedom is virtually nonexistent for a lot of American kids today. We bemoan the fact kids spend too much time inside, on screens and overscheduled with after-school activities. But we are unwilling to take the risk of just letting them run free. Despite the fact that kidnappings are at an all-time low, caregivers have been arrested for letting their children go to the park or wait in the car unchaperoned. Logically I think most of us know the child will be safe, but because our culture highlights and saturates us with stories of tragedy, we are much more likely to err on the side of caution and not let them play outside with friends and strangers.

And our fear does not just curtail our freedoms and the freedoms of our personal families. When people let fear take over and mistakes are made, it is often the people most marginalized by society who are most put at risk. The news and our social media feeds are rife with tales of mistakes made by people driven by fear. The white woman who called the police on a black man walking into his own apartment because her fear, driven by racism, drove her mistake. Luckily no one was hurt in that instance, but I have no doubt you can recall too many tragedies where someone of privilege let fear drive them in a way that led to accidental harm to someone less privileged. This happens in the world of adults daily. However, it also happens in our schools.

Recently I was in a school where three boys ages eight to ten got into an altercation in the lunchroom. There was an argument regarding who left something on top of one boy's lunch and it spiraled. One of the boys was much bigger than the others. One of them had much darker skin than the other two. None of the three boys were white, but they all experienced a range of privilege based in part on shade of skin color as well as size and socioeconomics. The principal, a Black woman with decades of experience in the public school system, said that as part of their work in a restorative circle she wanted the kids to understand that it was very important to never assume or accuse someone of something but especially a person of color. "I told them, I'm just being honest with you, if you are wrong the consequences are way higher. As boys of color you should know that." All three boys could have been responding with fear of each other for a variety of reasons.

[handwritten marginalia:] How do we know racism was involved? Assumption — Boys + girls fight regardless of skin color —

One was bigger and more physically powerful than the others. One came from a much wealthier family who was very involved in the school in a visible way. One was seen as popular. Each of them, like many of us, could have been affected by colorism, or the idea of judging someone based on the darkness or lightness of their skin. Each of the boys had their own reasons to fear the power the others had over them. That fear made it difficult for each of them to think calmly because so much felt like it was in play and at risk. What the boys were not afraid of in that moment, but the principal brought into sharp relief, was the larger consequences that could befall them if this skirmish had happened in a different context. They might have been afraid of each other in small and large ways, but that was nothing compared to the way larger society might treat them. And by allowing their personal fear to dictate their actions, they were not taking that larger, and likely scarier context, into account.

When I heard the principal discuss her work with those boys, I was struck by how different her response was from others in authority. I knew she had received training in restorative justice and had asked her staff to do the same. I knew that she had read and trained in culturally relevant pedagogy and was currently studying trauma-informed instruction. I also know that her own identity as a Black woman, who grew up in the public school system, first as a student, then a teacher, then an assistant principal, and finally a principal, brought with it a rich array of lived and learned experiences. She saw the boys in their identities. She named the power of fear as well as race in making the mistakes that led to the skirmish. And she set them up for understanding their own responsibility in not perpetuating fear-based mistakes as well as helping them to understand how, through no fault of their own, they might be on the receiving end of a fear-based mistake in the future.

The cafeteria incident ended well. But I can imagine, and I am sure you can too, a thousand other times and places where it wouldn't or didn't. This is in no small part because when anyone is mistakenly accused of something, the accused must rely on the person in power's good will and character. In the case of the boys in the cafeteria, the principal is driven by an educational and life philosophy steeped in antiracism. But not everyone is so fortunate to find themselves at the mercy of one who benevolently wields their authority. Although this is something educators who want the best for the young people in our care should be concerned about in terms of the world outside our own classrooms, we also need to take an honest look at our own roles as authorities. Teachers wield the largest power in our students' school days. In some cases that power follows them out of the school building and to wherever they go after school. When we look at educators' power over students' time (scheduling the school day, assigning homework, complicating or simplifying tasks), confidence (compliments, sarcasm, creating assignments that are accessible or not, grading), and future (teaching the content needed for future learning, offering the appropriate levels of support or independence for mastery, advice, letters of recommendation), it is easy to see why and how a student might be affected by that fear. Although more and more teachers are working to actively dismantle power structures in school that induct students into and perpetuate systems of inequity, the current fact remains that despite some of our difficulty in owning it, teachers hold more power than students. The power discrepancy in teaching—that teachers hold power over students—requires constant self-vigilance. Although sometimes, if we're honest, we can admit we have moments of fear of our students—whether it's fear that we'll never be able to get that one kid to calm down, or whether we have fear of physical danger from students who struggle with self-regulation, we can find ourselves forgetting our own power and allowing fear to be a mistake-prone driver of our actions. How much is our fear impacting our students? See Figure 4-2 for some tools to examine our fear in constructive ways.

Examining How Much We've Internalized Cultural Fears

	Restorative Justice Resources
How do we react to misbehavior in our classroom?	**REL Northwest:** https://ies.ed.gov/ncee/edlabs/regions/northwest/askarel/restorative-justice.asp **Edutopia:** https://www.edutopia.org/blog/restorative-justice-resources-matt-davis **Children's Defense Fund:** https://www.childrensdefense.org/wp-content/uploads/2018/06/restorative-justice-resource.pdf
	Social Emotional Learning and Equity
Do we have positive relationships with all of our students? What do we notice about the ones we don't have positive relationships with?	• **CASEL:** https://casel.org/csi-resources-equity/ • **Teaching Tolerance:** https://www.tolerance.org/node/116585 • **GLSEN:** https://www.glsen.org/ *Culturally Responsive Teaching & The Brain,* Zaretta Hammond (2014) *Stamped from the Beginning,* Ibram X. Kendi (2016) *My Grandmother's Hands,* Resmaa Menakem (2017) *Why Are All the Black Kids Sitting Together in the Cafeteria?* 2nd ed., Beverly Daniel Tatum (2017)

Figure 4-2 **Examining How Much We've Internalized Cultural Fears**

Helping Students with Their Fear

Since our students' fears both inside and outside of school can have a direct impact on learning, it feels less helpful to categorize their fears. Suffice it to say, like us, students worry about being alone and their physical safety. They also have fears that have to do with security. Fears stemming from rich imaginations are not unheard of and difficult to anticipate. Not all fears will play a role in school nor need to be addressed unless they are somehow impeding their school or life. According to Dr. Rachel Busman of the Child Mind Institute, there are a few steps adults can take to support a child experiencing fear:

- Validate that the fear is valid, but don't linger. For example: "You look like you're feeling uncomfortable. Like maybe you're afraid. It's OK to feel afraid right now."

- Make a plan with the child for how to handle that fear. For example: "Although taking tests can feel scary, there are ways you can help yourself feel less afraid. One way is to give yourself enough time to prepare for the test through review and study. Another is to do something to help yourself feel better physically— like taking a walk or taking deep breaths."

- Be patient and encouraging as the child works through that plan. For example: "I see you. And I know you did a lot of work reviewing. So what else can you do to help that fear back off a bit?"

But of course, this isn't always possible to do for every student or sometimes even what's preferable. "Fears that don't interfere with a child's life don't always need getting over," said Dr. Busman. As we watch our students learn and get to know what works or doesn't work for maximizing their learning, a wise teacher is attuned to when a child experiences fear in a way that holds back learning. In particular, we want to notice when the fear overrides the conscious mind and makes it impossible for the student to think and more likely to make unproductive mistakes. And in our more reflective moments we might admit that we too have moments of fear that get in the way of our own learning and growth.

STORY EDITING FEAR AND MISTAKES

Much has been written about the transformative power of story. In one of my favorite studies, researchers looked at children who become more resilient and successful than others and the family narratives they were told growing up (Fivush, Bohanek, and Duke 2008). They categorized the three main types of family narratives in this way:

- *Ascending narratives:* These are stories about past relatives and how they started at the bottom and moved to their current higher status. These stories may focus on luck, hard work, or some other family value as the reason the family's fortunes grew and changed.

- *Descending narratives:* These stories are about how a family was once higher status than they are now, but through bad luck or bad choices is now at a lower status than relatives from long ago.

- *Oscillating narratives:* These stories tell the story about how a family has had up-and-down periods—times of struggle and times of triumph and times of setback followed by upswings.

The researchers discovered that the kind of family narrative regularly told to children was a great predictor of their emotional health and happiness. Knowing the premise of this book, it should come as no surprise to you that the oscillating narrative was correlated with the most positive results. The embracing of fear, setbacks, and mistakes as part of a typical life's journey and telling these moments as stories is a powerful and healthy way to support our students. By looking for those opportunities when students experience and then overcome their fears and helping them to mold those into narratives that they either tell or write, we are helping students to develop a habit that will serve them long after they have left us.

Of course, just telling those up-and-down stories would not be enough when we are taking a cold hard look at not only fear, but the mistake consequences that often travel with fear. We need to look at the way those stories are cast and the work we can do to mine them for every possible shred of empowerment.

In *Redirect: Changing the Stories We Live By*, Timothy Wilson (2015) explores the science and theory behind the power of personal narratives as a way to understand and shape human lives. In particular he discusses the role of the way we tell stories and how they help us make meaning as well as purpose out of the events that occur in our lives. He introduces the idea of story editing, a powerful tool that could be used to help teachers and caregivers, as well as ourselves, look at adverse situations and imbue them with meaning and purpose. He points to situations where people were able to grapple with difficult circumstances such as cancer diagnosis or lost jobs, positively and with forward motion, by doing the work of story editing—looking at the events that occurred in a story.

This makes me think about our students and our own perspectives when faced with fear-based mistakes. We know that if our situation is fear driven, our conscious mind is turned off, making some of the reflective work needed in the moment all but impossible to do. However, by adapting Wilson's idea of story editing, we can guide ourselves, and our students, when the fear is not present to story edit and create meaning, purpose, and hope for change. And in that way, we are also leaning on Fivush, Bohanek, and Duke's narrative work as well, by tapping the oscillating narrative in the process.

STORY EDITING IN THE CLASSROOM

I could imagine story editing going many different ways in the classroom. That said, I wouldn't recommend trying it unless you know your students very well and have knowledge of trauma responsive practices. When done with a light and cautious touch, this can be a power-building experience for students; however, I could also imagine it to be triggering if not done with the utmost caution.

You could start with asking students to think of a time that they felt a small fear. You could do this as a whole-class lesson or just working with a few students in particular who are finding fear to be an obstacle to their learning.

Next, you can model by telling a story of your own fear or sharing one you wrote down. It does not matter if you are a writing teacher or not; in fact, science educators who wrote *The Stories of Science* (MacNeil, Goldner, and London 2017) give us many compelling reasons that storytelling in all subject areas, including and especially science, is a vital tool educators should employ more often. You might write or tell the story like a fully crafted narrative, complete with setting, action, and dialogue. This story does not need to end well. In many ways the best candidates for practicing story editing are ones that did not go well so that there's more to practice on. You might write something like this:

> *One night, when I was your age, my mom asked me to take the laundry down to the laundry room in my apartment building. I went downstairs, but I was the only one there. It was dark and quiet. I heard a sound I wasn't expecting and my heart started to pound. I threw the laundry in the machine. Then all of the sudden the lights went off! I screamed. I couldn't breathe. I didn't even turn the machine on. I just started running. As I did, the lights went back on and I remembered they were on a sensor.*

If the students feel comfortable telling or writing their own story, make space for that. But avoid making it a "must-do" task, and know that many students will learn a lot just through your modeling. After the storytelling, as part of the revision process, model for them with your story or prompt them to think of the possible reasons things happened as they did as well as other ways to give the event more meaning.

- What can you/they learn from the events in the story?

- Even if things went badly, especially if they did, are there ways that fear can have good aspects?

- How can the story end with an element of hope?

Model folding those things into the story and if students did choose to work on their own stories, coach them in ways to include them. Model ways of reimagining moments of the story so that the story goes in a more meaningful way or there are lessons to take away that will help you (or them) better respond if a similar situation was to arise in the future.

One night my mom asked me to take the laundry down to the laundry room in my apartment building. I knew my mom was exhausted from work and she always does so much for us so I was happy to help out, even though going to the basement is not my favorite thing. I went downstairs, but I was the only one there. It was dark and quiet. I decided to take a deep breath and even said to myself, "It's fine. Everything is fine." Then I heard a sound I wasn't expecting and my heart started to pound. But I talked to myself again and said, "Listen, you're feeling a little nervous so any sound is going to make you a little jumpy. But you're in an old building and old buildings are noisy." My heart slowed down a bit so I threw the laundry in the machine. Then all of the sudden the lights went off! I screamed. But then all at once I felt so silly. I remembered all at once that the lights were on a sensor. So I waved my hands over my head and the room flooded with light again.

After students get a chance to consider a nonacademic fear, break down the steps for them and show them how they can use those same steps in academic situations they might fear such as giving an in-class presentation, taking a test, or some other school-based challenge, making sure to always ground it in your own examples.

Opening Possibilities by Letting Go

Adina, a veteran kindergarten teacher in Brooklyn, said she was afraid of curriculum night every year. Every year she stood in front of the parents and caregivers and presented the curriculum in "stand and deliver" style. "It never went well. I was super formal. The grown-ups all sat in the tiny chairs while I stood up. People tuned me out. It felt unnatural and uncomfortable."

Then one year, Adina admitted to herself the reason she kept doing curriculum conferences this way was because she was afraid of what the adults might think. She wanted to assert herself as the authority, but she also felt like she was creating a distance between herself and the caregivers. "Then one day I went to a mindfulness workshop and the presenter had us all sit on the floor with her. And she sat on the floor. And there was such a sense of community and togetherness that I realized I needed to make a change. I let go of my fear, and instead, gathered all the families onto the rug with me. We all sat in a circle and it changed everything. Everyone was tuned in. We were all on the same team. And it was the best conference yet. And that fear of mine? Completely gone."

Adina decided not only to reflect on a practice that wasn't working, but also to look closely at how fear was the catalyst of that mistake. So often when we make mistakes, we focus on the moment of the mistake and the aftermath. We work to fix whatever is broken when we can. I think is important to note that Adina stepped back and looked past the action that was the mistake to the cause of that action: fear. Even after years of doing something the same way, even when the fear had become almost ignorable and sort of acceptable, she took the bold step of admitting that something that could have been just one of the parts of teaching she didn't feel great about was something worth admitting she was mistaken about. And that mistake was driven by fear. Perhaps not a serious fear, but big enough to affect her actions.

What Adina did reminds us to look more closely at the whole of our practice. To look for places that aren't going as well as they could be, and to take the brave step of asking ourselves if the reason that is so is because of a mistake. And then to take the next step after that and ask if there is a mistake, is that mistake driven by fear? I would be willing to wager that for many of us, in the course of a day, week, or even year of teaching, we can point to a significant number of our errors, or even our students' errors, that are driven by fear. By knowing it, expecting it, and naming it, we can go a long way toward reducing mistakes.

COMMON COGNITIVE ERROR

"Everything Will Be OK"

You may or may not know that the U.S. Food and Drug Administration has a set standard of how many bugs and bug parts can be included in ketchup and still be sold. But it's not only ketchup. The FDA puts out a whole handbook on the topic: *Food Defects Levels Handbook* (U.S. Food and Drug Administration). The premise is that no food is perfect, and we will have contaminations. So we have to set a level of defect or contamination that is acceptable. Which means that curious minds like mine can look up their favorite food and discover what kind of defect is allowed and the amount:

- Chocolate can contain the following: insect filth, rodent filth, and shells from the cocoa nibs. *Spoiler alert:* Less than 1 rodent hair per 100 grams of chocolate is acceptable.
- Coffee beans can contain the following: insect filth and mold. An average of 10 percent or more is not acceptable.
- Pepper, whole black can contain insect filth, mammalian excreta, and foreign matter. But not more than 1 percent.

The point of this is not to put you off your lunch, but rather to point out that people have created measures and systems that decide what level of error we are willing to accept. Yes, bugs are a natural part of farming. But, if we can pull enough bugs and other detritus out that we can set a percentage of acceptability, that means we actually know the level where could be harm done. I can't help but wonder how the FDA established those levels. I imagine scientists sitting and dropping a single rodent hair into a bottle of ketchup and a green light flashing. Then that same scientist dropping another single strand of rodent hair into the bottle and a red light flashing as the bottle gets sucked down a chute to be disposed of. At what level is the level of error too much to accept? It feels a little jarring to even consider.

The FDA's *Food Defect Levels Handbook* seems like a farcical level of detail about acceptable mistakes, but when you think about what those guidelines prevent, well, I raise my can of tomato juice (with no more than ten fly eggs, five fly eggs and one maggot, or two maggots per 100 grams) to them and the bacterial poisoning they prevent (U.S. Food and Drug Administration 2005).

Yes, it is true that very many defects are completely fine. We can acknowledge that we all literally, and figuratively, eat a little excrement, but that doesn't mean that we should embrace the idea that eating excrement is OK. There are many, many mistakes that really will not affect the big picture. And stopping at every little mistake or pausing before every action to consider every possible mistake you need to avoid can prevent us from getting anything done. Every teacher has had students who are so fearful of mistake-making that they freeze up and can't actually do what they need to do. And our job is to help those students understand that the mistakes in this learning environment will not cause anyone harm.

Unfortunately, for many of us, a common cognitive error can stem from generalizing that idea, especially when it comes to teaching. Just because some errors happen and everything is still fine does not mean that all levels of errors are acceptable. Deciding what's an acceptable level of error is an essential part of our job as teachers—What can we decide is no big deal? What realm of student mistakes can we let next year's teacher address?

When I think of mistakes in the world that felt like a minor thing but then later resulted in tragedy, the first one that comes to mind is the *Challenger* disaster. Carrying a team of astronauts and a school teacher, who planned to teach lessons to students on Earth from orbit, the *Challenger* exploded at seventy-three seconds into its flight, killing all on board. For those of us who had watched and celebrated this learning mission, it was a devastating event. A long investigation identified the explosion's cause as an O-ring seal on the rocket booster that had been compromised by the extreme cold weather during the launch. NASA engineer Roger Boisjoly had warned that the seals were less than perfect and could malfunction under the expected cold conditions of the planned launch, but the decision was made that the seals were good enough. They weren't. The level of defect passed the acceptable mark and lives were lost. Everything was not OK.

Consuming rat excrement in ketchup and losing the lives of seven human beings are vastly different examples of the consequences of mistake acceptance, but they do help us evaluate our own acceptance of error. Are we able to think through possible outcomes in a way that ensures right action? Clearly, accepting mistakes without any effort at prevention is just as problematic as being bogged down by every possible error. However, even within the safer middle ground zone, there are places where we as educators stumble when deciding which mistakes really will end up being OK and which can be catastrophic.

What "Everything Will Be OK" Sometimes Really Means

Comparing teaching mistakes to catastrophe feels pretty heavy-handed, I know, especially because we already feel too much unreasonable pressure to fix problems that are outside of our control. I'm not trying to frighten people with possible outcomes but to instead question the stance we sometimes adopt. Although "everything will be OK" is sometimes true, it isn't always, and if we're not mindful of when we say that, it might become our default stance of disengagement.

I think "everything is OK" is a go-to response of some educators because of how overwhelmed we feel by the conditions of teaching today. Too much responsibility and too little support can leave us with a strong awareness of our own limitations that we surrender to the bit of magical thinking that everything will be OK regardless of whether we do anything or not. We can disassociate ourselves from the problem if we decide that everything will work itself out ("I don't need to really get all that involved. I'm not really that connected to it anyway."). But the mistakes we ignore can turn into the problems other colleagues, or our students themselves, have to solve later. "Everything will be OK" can be a self-comforting wish statement when we want to look at something from a comforting distance. We don't want to get any closer to it because it's threatening in some way. If we self-monitor for that kind of distancing, we might bring a little more attention to it to realize that what's really behind "everything is OK" is instead "this is too overwhelming for me to deal with right now." I think teachers often make this statement when they face a systemic issue that feels too large for them, like a teacher realizing how many of their students cheated on their final papers. Instead of questioning what's behind the cheating, the teacher gives the students the option to rewrite or fail and thinks "everything will be OK moving forward" without ever addressing the cause of the cheating. The teacher chooses that path rather than investigating what went wrong and doesn't uncover students' resentment about being told what they have to read or that their lack of under-standing about the content drove their decision to cheat. When we find ourselves thinking "everything will be OK," perhaps instead we need to develop a stance of inquiry and ask, "What's not OK right now? Why?" Asking those questions first and foremost honors our own discomfort and then helps us get at the truth of the situation. This suspicious, some-what pessimistic stance can feel disorienting for some. Especially if you tend toward the optimistic end of the glass-filling metaphor. How can you manage the middle road of not accepting everything is OK but neither assuming that every mistake needs to be corrected at that moment?

Bringing a Sense of Inquiry to What Isn't OK

Even though all mistakes provide information, it is also true that all the information we are gaining from some mistakes does not need to be addressed. Time or self-realization might work to turn that mistake into a learning experience or else the mistake is not of enough consequence to warrant an intervention. Some things truly are developmental, such as:

- pronouncing the /w/ sound for /l/ in early childhood—like a kid saying *wittle* for *little*

- struggling with the concept of long division in third grade

- choosing to complete an assignment in a way suggested by middle school peers, rather than the way outlined by the teacher, and getting a poor score

- refusing to do work or cheating on work (and reaping the negative effects) that feels assigned more for expectations of compliance than personal growth—a common choice of adolescents.

Some things do work themselves out or will be OK. If we step in too quickly, we could quash the independence and agency of a student who would otherwise figure things out on their own. For many students, and in many situations with more experience and practice, lots of mistakes will work themselves out. Additionally, ruling out good, devel-opmental, and unimportant mistakes right away helps us to focus on the mistakes that do require us to step in. The crucial thing for educators to decide upon is when that mistake needs to be watched more carefully and mindfully so that it doesn't become something larger. It can be helpful to create a framework when studying student errors. Here's one option: Figure 5-1.

Step 1: Identify the point of error.

Step 2: Understand the context of the error.

Step 3: Consider the potential harm that could happen if there is no response from a teacher.

Some questions that can help illuminate the context of the error:

- What do I know about this student?
- Is this mistake recurrent?
- Does it affect their learning, others' learning, or their emotional/physical safety?
- Is the mistake on something that is a foundational skill, upon which other skills build?
- Is this something that this student just needs more time and practice with?
- Does the student seem "trapped" by a negative behavior pattern?
- Could the content around the mistake be taught in another way?

Figure 5-1 Deciding Whether to Address a Student Mistake

Acknowledging that some mistakes can fall into the "need to be addressed" category is important. Certain aspects of teaching and learning can get seriously detoured if not irreparably harmed when mistakes are allowed to continue without intervention. Often students' behavioral mistakes are punished but not addressed or simply overlooked. For example, the emotional vocabulary of some students, often but not only boys, is limited to two "strong" emotions—happiness or anger. Outbursts of anger are punished but considered normal. So instead of recognizing and addressing the reality that many students are often not given the space to address other emotions, we encourage them in the behaviors that disassociate them from their real feelings. When we witness a student experiencing frustration, and then just as quickly see them tamp it down, we might compliment them. When we see a child expressing sadness, then wiping away tears quickly, we might give a quick pat on the shoulder and a thumbs up. We see the results of our reactions to this as "everything will be OK"—children who become adolescents and then adults who are lonely *α*

Sadness

loneliness

and lost given the clear message that <u>disassociation is better than appropriate</u> expression. They can become more subject to the negative cultural narratives of dominance, in some cases acting this out through violence or sexual oppression. If we as teachers can acknowledge that everything will not always be OK, we create space to address the problems too many others have overlooked.

And of course, emotions are not the only thing we can put into "everything will be OK" thinking. Reading is an essential skill and its teaching is loaded with things we can decide are OK that aren't. One common example is when students miscue based on context but overlook phonics. For example, a student is reading a picture book and encounters the word *floor*. The student consults the picture and then reads *ground*. Often teachers of students who are newer readers might be tempted to let this error go. After all, it's clear the student is using a lot of information. The student clearly understands the sentence meaning and syntax. However, if the teacher does not coach into the student attending to the letters, the possible impact of the mistake grows exponentially. Surely one miscue is not a problem. But if session after session sitting beside the teacher the student reads this way, the teacher's inattention to the error implies that decoding is not all that important. The child might not be aware of the mistake, which is one sort of wrinkle. But, the impact of allowing that error to continue without guidance becomes even more problematic if the child is aware that they substituted a word based on meaning rather than letters. Many students leave school without being fluent readers so believing that everything will be OK is not only foolish, but also possibly dangerous. If the student has a pattern of not using decoding strategies when reading, this might be a red flag that there is an underlying reading disorder that needs to be addressed.

In this instance, the point of error was the miscue of a substitution based on meaning and not phonics. Understanding how regularly this error occurs (one time, occasionally, or all the time) is the key to knowing how or if to respond. And, if this is a regular error, the potential for harm is actually fairly high. Because of that, I would be vigilant for any repeats.

We can look at another example from mathematics. Whether you have been teaching for thirty years or three, the chances are pretty good that the way students learn math is markedly different than the way you learned it in school. We have learned from a range of mathematicians that an overemphasis on answers and an underemphasis on conceptual understanding and process are problematic. So the work that's done in class and taken home often <u>emphasizes process over answer</u>. And, if media posts are to be believed, parents and caregivers across the country are aghast at this drastic change. If you are a teacher who assigns math homework, it would be rare indeed if you have not yet seen an assignment, carefully designed for the student to practice problem-solving and conceptual know-how, return from home with only the answers written down when it is returned. If work is shown, it is almost always in an algorithm that focuses less on meaning than speed.

Partially

Many of us might shrug our shoulders and say, "It's fine. It was at home. He'll eventually understand the concept, so it won't matter." And, although it's true that is possible, it is also true that the home adult's different approach could be fine if the child understands that people do math differently but also understands that knowing things conceptually is important. However, we don't always know that. It is also entirely possible that the adult at home is not only unclear about how math is taught, but also is developing a grave dislike for it. Students in this position might inadvertently get the message that school and home are not in partnership and therefore not feel that it truly is important to understand math as long as the answer is "correct." Since there is no way to know for sure, perhaps taking a less optimistic view would be better for learning. Instead of trusting it will all be OK if we just let it be, we could ask families to come in for a night to teach them how math is taught now or send home links to flipped math lessons that show those methods alongside a letter explaining the shifts in math instruction or invite families to join a committee on math instruction to help build some bridges, which might go a long way toward strengthening not only the home and school connection, but also the coherence of instruction for the student.

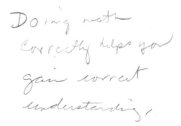

Doing math correctly helps you gain correct understanding.

SINCE THERE IS NO WAY TO KNOW FOR SURE, PERHAPS TAKING A LESS OPTIMISTIC VIEW WOULD BE BETTER FOR LEARNING.

In this example, the first step is to acknowledge that the error is in the lack of showing of work. Why? Is it because there is an adult at home helping? Is it because the student is choosing to do the work differently for another reason? The answers to those questions will help to work on step 2. If there is a simple explanation and the student truly does understand how to do the work but is doing it differently because that's how Mom prefers it's done, then this is probably a good case of letting well enough alone. The context of this has a huge impact as to whether or not real harm can or would be done if the error is not addressed.

These are two of many examples reminding us that everything will not always be OK. Some mistakes need our immediate attention.

It can be dangerous to assume the best will happen, so as teachers we should maintain an awareness of the kinds of learning mistakes that require immediate attention and the ones we can leave well enough alone. See Figure 5-2 for some examples.

Responses to Student Mistakes and Mistake Prevention

• *Acknowledge that the mistakes we note send just as powerful of a message as the ones we ignore.* Educators make decisions all day long. So much so that researchers have even studied us for decision fatigue. Part of our daily decision-making process includes which mistakes we will focus on and which we can safely ignore. Regardless as to our final decision, it is important to remember that the mistakes our students know we witnessed, or made ourselves, and how we respond to them (or don't respond) send a message whether we intend it to or not. If we always comment on a computation error but never on a conceptual one, students might infer one matters more to us than the other. Our choices are always being observed, even a simple move such as saying, "I see what happened there, but that's not where we should be focused right now. If it turns out this work is staying, we can go back and work on that. What really matters right now is . . ."

• *Research important milestones, values, and competencies.* When try-ing to determine whether or not to intervene, it helps a lot to know if there are milestones, values, or competencies that students need to know in a certain progression or within a certain time frame. So for example, for years I did not say too much about my students' pen grip. I assumed they would get it eventually. But when an occupational therapist explained that pen grip becomes permanent for most kids by the middle of second grade, I knew that when working with grades younger than that I needed to be more proactive in correcting it. In grades older than that I might need to work on efficiency strategies or maybe even moving into digital tools if the grip is becoming an obstacle. There are milestones, values, and competencies that have a range of time where things work best and when they are unlikely to work well. Knowing these helps me to prioritize what I should push and when, as well as helping me decide what to let go of for now. Things like development of read-ing skills, math conceptual understandings, scientific concepts, and more can have very clear guidelines. Depending on the grade or discipline you teach, you might decide to even create a cheat sheet to help keep you aware of any possible red flags. See Figure 5–3.

- **Determine whether something is load bearing or not.** Even if something does have a time frame, not everything is of equal value. For example, I've been informed that if I wanted to become a serious gymnast, I should have started as a young child. I could still take gymnastics, of course, and learn to swing around on a pommel horse, but the time I could have become a serious competitor has passed. Not all milestones are created equally. When considering which mistakes to address, consider not only the skill but also its overall value to the student, subject, and long-term success. Some skills and understandings become the load-bearing walls that hold up the whole house. Others can be ignored or allowed to crumble without major effect on the whole structure. We want to separate out the load-bearing mistakes from the nonload-bearing and then prioritize accordingly. See Figure 5–3 for learning and developmental milestones by age.

Figure 5-2 **Responses to Student Mistakes and Mistake Prevention**

Some Learning and Developmental Milestones by Age

Ages	Reading	Writing	Math
By end of kindergarten	• Identify beginning, middle, and ending sounds of words heard spoken. • Match simple words they hear to ones they see on the page. • Sound out simple words. • Predict what happens next in a story.	• Know the sounds letters make. • Spell words based on the sounds. • Label pictures with a few words. • Write simple sentences.	• Add by counting on fingers on one hand, up to five, and starting at six on the next hand. • Identify the larger of two numbers up to twenty. • Copy or draw symmetrical shapes. • Follow multistep instructions with words like *first* and *next*.

continues

Ages	Reading	Writing	Math
Grades 1–2	• Increase number of words they recognize by sight. • Improve reading speed and fluency. • Go back and reread a word or sentence that doesn't make sense. • Connect what they're reading to their lives, other books, or the bigger world.	• Hold pencil in tripod grip. • Form letters correctly. • Spell correctly some common words that are spelled irregularly (sight words). • Write a simple story from their lives. • Write a simple informational piece about something they learned.	• Predict what comes next in a pattern. • Count to 100 using ones, twos, fives, and tens. • Do basic addition and subtraction up to twenty. • Recognize and know the value of coins. • Read and make a simple bar chart.
Grades 3–5	• In grade 3 move from learning to read to reading to learn. • Accurately read words with more than one syllable. • Learn and understand prefixes and suffixes. • Identify and describe story elements (plot, characters, setting). • Make inferences. • Identify main theme.	• Spell words using roots, suffixes, prefixes, and other patterns. • Write using a variety of sentences, including complex sentences. • Understand and use a writing process for writing (rehearsing, drafting, revising, editing). • May use sources outside self for writing (references, quotes, etc.).	• Do addition and subtracting with regrouping (grade 3). • Know how to multiply and divide using fact families (grade 3). • Write and compare fractions and decimals on a number line. • Use more than one way to solve a problem. • Estimate and round. • Complete long division.
Middle school	• Expand vocabulary to understand more complex texts. • Identify minor themes. • Analyze story elements, such as how characters develop. • Identify imagery and symbolism.	• Continue to develop typing skills, grammar, and vocabulary. • Write more complex narratives from personal experiences. • Write argumentative pieces including claims, reasons, and evidence. • Cite sources in informational and argumentative pieces.	• Begin basic algebra. • Graph ordered pairs. • Work with fractions, percentages, and proportions. • Use formulas to figure out complicated problems and to find area, perimeter, and volume of shapes.

Ages	Reading	Writing	Math
High school	• Determine themes and how they develop across the text. • Use text evidence to support analysis. • Analyze, synthesize, and evaluate ideas from the text. • Understand irony, sarcasm, satire, and understatement.	• Develop keyboarding, grammar, and vocabular skills more. • Write in a range of genres on a range of topics and disciplines. • Use strategies for finding, selecting, and combining resources from a variety of sources. • Develop sophisticated revision strategies.	• Use numbers in real-life situations (such as comparing student loan rates). • Use mathematical language to convey thoughts and solutions. • Begin to see how mathematical ideas build upon each other. • Use maps, graphs, or other representations to learn and convey information.

Figure 5-3 **Some Learning and Developmental Milestones by Age**

Reducing the Chance of Mistakes to Almost Zero

For some students, and in some situations, we really cannot make a mistake. The stakes are just too high. And when that is the case, we can and might consider going to extreme measures to re-create the conditions my friends in the military have called "zero-fail missions." These are missions of such import that lives, billions of dollars, or even the very survival of a republic are at stake. When those missions take place, whether it is to capture an enemy, reclaim a military base, or rescue important assets, the team members involved in those missions know from the outset that they must operate with precision and minimize the opportunities for errors.

You might be sitting there thinking, "Hmm—I know teaching is already pretty high pressure—but military level?" You might be wondering if I'm suggesting you put on camo, clutch a knife in your teeth, and rappel down a cliff. Well, for the most part, I'm not suggesting that. Most of the time in teaching, the choices we make and the mistakes we risk do not literally call for life-or-death precision. But I can think of many times, and I am sure you can too, where we simply cannot fail and we need to put ourselves in a position to make failure the least likely to happen.

Some examples of classroom-type zero-fail missions include a student learning to read, returning to the school after a field trip with all of your students, ensuring that a student with an individualized education plan program gets all the services and accommodations on that program. If you're anything like me, you try not to think too much about any of the regular zero-fail missions you face regularly. You might duck your head and run straight into them instead, then realize afterward that you were holding your breath the whole time. As a New York City school teacher I never relaxed when it came to subway field trips. No matter how many chaperones I had or how short the trip, preparing to take thirty-two students onto crowded subway cars, with transfers, during rush hour, was not something to take lightly. And every time I did it, I was like one of those characters you see in military movies where there is a mission prep montage. I had diagrams, lists, rehearsals, even a big pep talk with myself and my class before we stepped foot out the door. And the whole time we were on our mission—er, field trip—I was as vigilant, barking, and frenetic as a military officer on a mission. At the time I didn't realize that I was doing all this because mistakes were not an option I wanted to even consider. But now, when I go on a field trip as a parent chaperone, I can't help but want to hug my sons' teachers as they do the same sorts of things.

Aiming to reduce or eliminate any chance of error, as you can well imagine, is not the easiest thing to do. Thinking things through like this is very labor-intensive. However, when failure is not a proverbial option, you can take steps to dramatically decrease the chance of making a mistake.

What are our zero-fail missions in teaching?

- ***Relationship Building:*** Every child feels cared for and respected by me, their teacher.

  How can I ensure zero-fail?

    - Get to know each individual through purposeful, positive interaction.
    - Self-assess my relationship with students on an ongoing basis.
    - Ask for help when needed. Ask trusted colleagues to observe my classroom interactions and give feedback on which students need more positive attention.

- ***Risk-Safe Community:*** Every child feels respected and cared for within our school and classroom community.

  How can I ensure zero-fail?

    - Teach how to be part of a community from day one. Make it a shared classroom inquiry with daily time for reflection. What are we noticing about ourselves as a community? What are we getting right? What do we need to do more of? Where are we struggling?

- Use restorative justice models that don't blame and shame individuals but focus on accountability and what's needed to move forward.

- Create space to talk about issues in the larger school community, and engage in dialogue with school leadership about important issues. *Homeroom*

- Ask for help when needed. Film or take notes on classroom interaction for later reflection. Ask trusted colleagues to observe students' interactions with each other and give feedback on which students need more positive attention.

- ***Positive Identity Building:*** Every child ends their time with me with an expanded, positive sense of self.

  How can I ensure zero-fail?

  - Make sure students see many different positive role models based on their identities—race, culture, and gender, sexuality, personality types, interests, and so on.

  - Create opportunities for students to have choice, to investigate their interests, and to reflect on their choices so that they start to see that "I'm the type of learner who . . ." and "I'm the type of person who . . ." Emphasize that our identities change and grow over time.

  - Ask for help when you're struggling. Find a like-minded colleague who will be your vulnerability buddy. Your school might not be a place you can share your struggles and be vulnerable but other people or places can be. For example, some make connections with colleagues miles away from them at conferences or institutes, make sure to exchange contact information, and set a regular time to talk. Many people have pseudonyms on Twitter and create professional learning communities there. Or if you'd rather not discuss things with another educators, try googling the issue and finding researchers who speak to what you're grappling with.

- ***Rigorous, Authentic Learning:*** Every child develops life and academic skills that ensure their success next year and the years beyond school.

  How can I ensure zero-fail?

  - Unpack learning expectations. What are the variety of ways and forms that this skill appears in the real world? Why is this expectation important? How can our classroom be a place for students to explore this skill in authentic, purposeful ways that help them see themselves as the adult scientists, writers, mathematicians, historians, artists?

- Make learning as universally accessible as possible and also differentiate learning when needed in meaningful, research-based ways.

- Ask for help when you're struggling. We all get trapped by the limits of our own imagination and sometimes need others' help to find a better path.

OK, ready? No, maybe not. Because although everything I just said might make good sense, it also might feel overwhelming. When we feel overwhelmed, everything is definitely not OK. On those days we swing wildly between wanting someone to just come and make all the decisions for us and wanting to believe if we smile and keep on keeping on everything will be OK. Those moments, sometimes whole days or longer, are when teacher decision fatigue has caught us. And although it's true that maybe that mistake we just made isn't terrible, maybe that one mistake is actually even OK, the larger truth is that our basic condition isn't OK. We are worn out and in danger of making more mistakes. More often than not when everything doesn't feel OK, some self-care is needed. If that's how you're feeling right now, go to Essay 3, even if you've already read it, and take a moment to do what's needed so that you are OK.

Resources for Rigorous Authentic Learning

Universal Design for Learning
Universal Design for Learning: Theory and Practice (2016) by Anne Meyer, David H. Rose, and David Gordon

Differentiation
How to Differentiate Instruction in Academically Diverse Classrooms (2017) by Carol Ann Tomlinson

Culturally Responsive Teaching
The Dreamkeepers (2009) by Gloria Ladson-Billings
Culturally Responsive Teaching and the Brain (2015) by Zaretta Hammond

Funds of Knowledge
Funds of Knowledge: Theorizing Practices in Households, Communities, and Classrooms (2005) edited by Norma González, Luis C. Moll, and Cathy Amanti

Inquiry
"Changing Hearts, Minds, and Actions Through Collaborative Inquiry" (2014) by Heidi Mills, Tim O'Keefe, Chris Hass, and Scott Johnson

THOMASSONS

Maintaining Mistakes for the Wrong Reasons

Mistakes Hide False Beliefs

A high school senior in Texas, Deandre Arnold had been growing his hair for years and tied it up so that he was following the school dress code of keeping it off his neck and ears. For some reason, in January 2020 this dress code changed, and he was informed by his Texas school district that unless he cut his hair, styled in dreadlocks, he would be suspended and not be allowed to walk at graduation. Deandre protested that it was part of his Trinidadian culture, even furnishing pictures of relatives who wear their hair in a similar style, but the district was not moved and refused to change the rule. When questioned about it, the district claimed the policy had been the same for thirty years, even though Deandre had been allowed to attend school with the exact same hairstyle without incident prior to January 2020.

People rallied around Deandre, including Black academics with dread-locks, celebrities, and eventually other schools that opened their doors to him. None of this moved the school district. In fact, even after it was pointed out that girls were allowed to have long hair as well as other boys and that every member of the district school board was white, the district doubled down and said it would absolutely not change its policy since it had been in place for thirty years.

RISK.
FAIL.
RISE.

Deandre

If you followed the story, you know Deandre ended up in a good place. His parents supported his decision. He left his school and enrolled in a new one where he was allowed to celebrate his culture and was invited to attend the Oscars with his mother as a guest of the team that produced the short film *Hair Love* (France 2020). There was a renewed focus on The Crown Act (CROWN Coalition 2019) recently passed in California to protect people from discrimination based on their natural hairstyles, which most often affects Black people, and if the law was passed in Texas, it most certainly would have protected Deandre.

But if you're like me, you don't just follow this story for Deandre, but also to learn from the school system's mistakes and how they responded. In this case, as of the writing of this book, the school district followed up their initial mistake of instituting a newly enforced dress code by suspending Deandre and denying him the privilege of walking at his graduation—they somehow made the initial mistake worse. When his family and then later supporters objected to it as being unfair and likely grounded in racism, the school district refused to concede or relax any parts of their dress code and instead later suspended Deandre's cousin Kaden Bradford for the same reason. Unfortunately, the trajectory that Barber Hill Independent School District took with their mistake-making is entirely familiar. It is very common for dress code policies to be designed with a particular image of academic propriety, usually upholding an image most commonly presented by white middle-class male students. When looking at dress code policies across the country, the violations most commonly listed describe fashion and hairstyles most commonly worn by people of color and girls. It is also appears that too many school administrations and districts rarely study their own implicit biases and then apply that self-knowledge to policy. Instead, they make policy based on a mistaken belief of "universal" academic decorum. Without reflection on where and how those policies emerged, many schools double down on these harmful decisions. They create apparatus to reinforce and maintain the mistake—new mandates, new punishments—that allow the false belief, in this case racism, to remain unchallenged. And so we see, again and again, in schools and other public institutions, that the public conversation becomes about someone not complying with something that is a mistake as a process of avoiding addressing the false belief.

This is a fairly common practice many of us engage in after making a mistake: not only don't we fix the mistake, we maintain it. We make actual efforts to create protective structures and almost beautify that mistake, almost like putting the mistake in a frame and hanging it on our living room walls. (Consider how often a dress code, for example, is described as part of "tradition.") These protective structures allow us to not examine anything problematic about our mistake and make us almost impervious to possible criticism. When we do not acknowledge or apologize for our mistake, but rather, like an embarrassed teenager who while trying to be cool walks into a wall and says, "I meant to do that," we start to believe our own claims and then feel completely justified in our errors.

Evaluate by Examining Purpose: Does Form Fit Function?

This idea—that we maintain mistakes so that we can avoid correcting a false belief—is a fairly new idea to me. I first heard about it from architecture, of all places. One of my friends is a city planner in DC and told me these kinds of mistakes you see in architecture have a name: Thomassons. The term was coined by the Japanese artist Genpei Akasegawa, who called elements in a city that were useless but nonetheless looked like conceptual artwork *hyperart* (Akasegawa 2010). He later specified a particular kind of hyperart as a *Thomasson*, describing architectural elements that are:

1. completely and utterly useless

2. being maintained.

Akasegawa named these pieces of hyperart after an American professional baseball player who played for the Tokyo Giants but got injured, so he sat out the rest of his contract on the bench. Completely useless. Maintained.

You recognize them when you see them. Although if you're anything like me, you didn't realize there was a name for them. Thomassons can be found in perfectly preserved signs for buildings that no longer (or never did) exist, doorways that lead to walls or nothingness, stairways that lead to nowhere. One of my favorites is an escalator that goes up a few feet into a wall. These are things whose original purposes have long been forgotten, maybe never even fulfilled, but somehow the object in question continues on. Very often they are mistakes in architecture that were never addressed. Someone built a staircase that was never in the blueprints. A door is cut into a third-floor room for a fire escape, but it was the wrong room. So now the door leads to nothing but air and is left that way. Sometimes, as the building or structure is renovated, particular elements are no longer needed but not removed—so what was originally something useful, like a window or a railing or a bridge, has now become a curious-looking mistake.

It's always interesting to me not just the uselessness of those doorways or windows or stairways, but rather the lengths that people will go to preserve them. What makes a Thomasson a Thomasson, and not just an unsightly anomaly, is the care they receive. They have a fresh coat of paint, potted flowers, shiny glass. Someone has looked at this unusable thing and decided not only "I'm not going to fix this" but also "I'm going to take care of it." There's actual effort involved—extra effort because the thing is not useable—to maintain this thing. Someone had to buy supplies and take time out of their life to preserve something that is problematic (Figure 6-1).

RISK.
FAIL.
RISE.

Figure 6-1 **Architectural Thomassons**

Thomassons remind me of so many things we do in teaching.

Such as that writing graphic organizer we introduce in September to help kids plan their stories. We are convinced that they will really love it. And they try it. But then eventually they stop using it. I stop teaching it. But I still keep photocopying it and putting it in the writing center. Sometimes I even insist that they use it, although there is no noticeable difference in their writing whether they use it or not. Useless. Maintained. Or that way we teach vocabulary, which is the way our childhood teachers taught us vocabulary. We tell students to use bigger words whether the words fit or not and to replace perfectly good words like *said* with words like *stated, mumbled,* and *declared,* even though we notice that professional writers almost exclusively use *said.* Even though we notice our kids keep using *said* or using those other words badly, we hang up a tombstone over our E-Board that says, *SAID IS DEAD.* And make a big bulletin board with synonyms of said. We know it doesn't feel right. We know it's not working. We know it's a mistake, yet we maintain it. We add the handrail to the useless staircase. See Figure 6-2.

I'd like you to stop for a few minutes and reflect a bit on one of your teaching Thomassons. Think of a practice or habit that you employ knowing that it's either wrong or just

Sample School Thomasson	Why It's Maintained	Why It's Problematic
Asking students to line up in boys' and girls' lines	It's a traditional and familiar way to manage groups of students.	It uses gender as a grouping factor when other less identity-laden ways that risk gender stereotyping of creating groups could be used.
Assigning and grading mandatory homework for students in grades K–5	Many families and teachers believe it is a good way to practice school skills, learn discipline, prepare for the work level in upper grades, and communicate with families.	There is scant research that shows K–5 students benefit from homework, and significant studies that show it can have a neutral or detrimental effect. There are also effective ways to meet the same goals without homework.
Starting the school day before 8:30 for adolescents	Many schools base their schedules on transportation demands, sports scheduling, and adult convenience.	Studies show that earlier start times have a negative impact on adolescent student learning because their sleep needs are different than students at different ages (Peltz et al. 2017).
Defending a classroom library, school booklist, or whole-class novel curriculum that does not include voices that have been marginalized	Educators get used to or attached to certain books, materials, or curricula. Or else there is a belief that certain texts are universal, despite those texts predominantly representing a small subsection of people, usually white and male.	Sims Bishop (1990), Tatum (2009), Ahmed (2018), and others' work has shown us the value of students seeing themselves and their identity reflected in the curriculum as well as being exposed to a wide range of identities different than themselves.
Using labels when speaking about students—"high flyers," "strugglers," "strivers," "IEP kids," "speds," "he's a J."	As educators we are often in a rush and using these terms turns into a shorthand when considering cohorts of kids and their needs.	This shorthand becomes a long-term label that later can morph into a deficit-based or narrow identity (Van Der Klift and Kunc 1994).

Figure 6-2 **Teaching Thomassons**

[Handwritten margin notes: Never label a student. Material is difficult for student. I meant worked hard they interpreted – too hard for me, can't do it.]

plain useless. This might be harder to do than it seems at first glance. As Carol Tavris and Elliot Aronson (2015) write in *Mistakes Were Made (but Not by Me)*, "Most people, when directly confronted by evidence that they were wrong do not change their point of view or plan of action but justify it more tenaciously" (2). We have a very hard time seeing when we make errors, and when we are confronted with indisputable errors, we reflexively justify our actions. So, this work of identifying a place where we are making a mistake can be daunting. Whether it is excusing myself for forgetting to pick up bread when my wife asked me too because I had so many other things on my mind, or spelling an author's name wrong on a citation (autocorrect!), I have realized I make a lot of excuses, or what Tavris and Aronson would call self-justifications.

Also, just to add to the fun, it can be even more difficult to know if something you're doing isn't working when you are building up stuff around it to make it appear OK.

So, if you're sitting there drawing a blank, I'd like to give you a few lenses to help you reflect. Study yourself for a day or ask a colleague to weigh in. You might even want to take low-inference notes for a day on everything you do and then reflect on it later when you're not with students. But because of how often teaching Thomassons are connected to a false belief, these can be very difficult to spot in ourselves. Often the most reliable path is to pay attention to our emotions in our teaching so that we can identify and challenge mistaken beliefs and replace them with accurate thinking. This process, pioneered by Albert Ellis (1997), Aaron and Judith Beck (2011), among others, is called *cognitive restructuring*. See Figure 6–3 for an example of how the cognitive restructuring process can help us spot our teaching Thomassons.

We know that repeated thought patterns create well-worn paths in the brain that we default to more easily than new thinking. When we're dismantling our Thomassons, it might be helpful to imagine the thinking as a major modern highway with all the tarmac, lighting, cement walls, and bridges that surround it. Taking that apart isn't a one-day project. This process is iterative: we repeat it, refining our positive belief statements and choosing wiser actions, until the negative emotions around the experience diminish significantly. Giving up a teaching Thomasson is not easy, even if it's a simple thing. When it seems simple, try envisioning your Thomasson as a sapling; it might look small, but the negative belief usually has strong roots. Again, that's why it's important we revisit our positive belief statements. They remind us to focus on behaviors that directly relate to that positive belief statement. The teaching Thomasson I am battling right now is a longstanding one. When I was growing up, I was explicitly taught that the male pronoun and form of words was the neutral. So, using *you guys* was something I grew up with and used with my students as a way of being less formal and more approachable. It felt less formal than *class* and less gendered than *boys and girls*. I know it's not accurate. I know some people really hate it, and it does the opposite of making me more approachable. Yet, for awhile, I sort of doubled down on it. I even used it fairly frequently in my social media posts as a way of personalizing them. I wouldn't be surprised if in at least one of my other books I have used it to address the reader. It has become so much a part of my banter and personality that it was very hard for me to stop. But it wasn't a one-time mistake that I just let go. I maintained. I used it again and again. Until one day I finally felt an uncomfortable feeling

1. **Pay attention to when you feel unpleasant emotions in your teaching or when you observe those emotions in your students.** Find a moment to write down or at least mentally identify which feeling you are experiencing most strongly. Stick to the big four negative emotions: anxiety, sadness, guilt/shame, and anger.	I feel angry and sad. Most students' final pieces of writing are not significantly different from their drafts. I've spent a lot of time on revision strategies, conferring with each student, and yet I'm still not seeing most students make their writing better.
2. **Identify the negative thought or belief most strongly related to your unpleasant feeling.** This belief is where we're stuck. It's a false belief that's perpetuating the mistake.	I believe that I've done everything I can and this either means that I'm incapable or it's the students' fault or maybe both.

3. **Recognize that your negative belief statement reflects a cognitive distortion/s:**
 	
    All-or-nothing
 	
    Jumping to conclusions
 	
    Labeling/mislabeling
 	
    Personalization
 	
    Selective attention
 	
    Overgeneralizing
 	
    Must/should/never catastrophizing
 	
    Emotional reasoning
	All-or-nothing
	
	Labeling/mislabeling

4. **Rewrite that negative belief as a positive belief.** This usually takes some revision as you may find yourself reintroducing cognitive distortions. Draft a few statements until you get to the one that feels the most true and useful to you. Try to keep it as short as possible. Hold on to this. Write it in a journal or on a sticky note. Revisit it when you feel stuck. This is what you know to be true.	My students and I are struggling with revision. I believe in the potential of my students as writers and of myself as a teacher of writing.
5. **Identify an action based on your positive belief.**	I need to talk with my students about how revision isn't working out as I'd hoped. I need to find out what they think, reflect on that, and see if I can change my process and supports to better speak to what their real needs are. I might not be sure, though, and may need to talk to other teachers or do some research on when students struggle with revision.

Figure 6-3 **Identifying and Challenging Teaching Thomassons**

I'd been living with for a bit and couldn't ignore it anymore: guilt. Then I had to stop and ask myself why. Why did I keep using a term that I knew was inaccurate and for many people offensive? Yes, of course I could take the point of view that I was falling victim to "political correctness," but as an educator who wants to connect with people, why on earth would I purposely use a phrase I know was a disconnection to many? The choice to do so was making me feel guilty, and I had to own that the reason was likely because I was making it an all-or-nothing thing. I either was informal and approachable with my students or I wasn't, and it felt like *you guys* was a primary way to do this. Also, I had personalized it so much that by admitting it was wrong, I would also have to admit I had messed up in front of all the students I had taught before.

I didn't stay too long in that reflection phase, remembering the research that tells us it's better to be forward looking (Haws 2015). So instead I imagined a future where my calling to people became an invitation, not a repeat exclusion. That helped a lot. I crafted a statement that rewrote my negative belief as a positive one. In this case it was, "I am struggling with using approachable language that is inclusive and gender neutral. I believe in my ability to be inclusive and my facility with language." Then I thought of how to replace or remove my own personal Thomasson. It was hard to just remove it. I needed to speak to groups of people fairly often. So instead I decided to replace it. I came up with some terms I liked better because they were more inclusive and still had that informal and approachable quality I was going for. So now I say, *friends, folx, y'all, everyone.*

A school I used to work with had a high percentage of students who came from communities that historically have been marginalized. Like many schools, they tried to keep a positive attitude about testing and used to regularly tell students they were going to do great on the annual state standardized tests. Although the students made some growth, it was incremental. This informal class-by-class cheering morphed into having regular test prep rallies complete with giant banners, chants, and an assembly. Students were cheered on to "Do your best and rock the test!" The rally was a loved event by many in the school community. Yet, the growth on the test result only moved incrementally. After a few years of holding the rally and handing out rubber motivational bracelets and practicing celebratory dances, the school paused when a student burst into tears during the test. The student confessed that they felt like they let the school down because even though they tried hard, the test still felt too hard and they didn't think they did well. When the teachers began to quietly ask other students about how they felt, teachers realized this student was not alone in feeling as if the rally was for someone else or as if something was wrong with them because they didn't think the test was all that doable.

What started as a well-meaning attempt to lift spirits and build confidence, which wasn't really effective, soon turned into something bigger and not only ineffective but also harmful. However, the thing that most impressed me was the teachers' and administrators' willingness to stop and reflect on the rally, even though it was a greatly loved event. So often the Thomassons that are the hardest for educators to let go of are the ones that feel fun, that they have been doing awhile, and that they have put a lot of work into. The test prep rally was all of the above.

For me, Thomassons are one of the most humbling types of mistakes that I make. Mainly because these are not one-time instances nor are they "innocent." I know better, and yet I keep repeating them. And then, the worst part for me, is that I go to the effort of protecting them. I can't leave well enough alone. Having a protocol and knowing that it is never too late for a do-over helps me avoid lingering too long on self-flagellation.

As we all look at our personal Thomassons and become more aware of the system-wide Thomassons, such as those maintained by Deandre Arnold's former school district, it is important to remember that no matter how long we have been making, maintaining, and defending mistakes, once we realize that we are mistaken, no matter how painful that realization is, it is time to rid ourselves of our Thomassons once and for all. In case you feel ready to do this work right now, Figure 6–4 lists some teaching Thomassons for further reflection.

Teaching Thomassons for Reflection

- Offering extrinsic rewards for cognitive tasks (like number of books read, test scores, mastering times tables, etc.)

- Punishing or rewarding students for behavior before teaching strategies for emotional and behavioral regulation

- Excusing the overrepresentation of white children and boys and underrepresentation of Indigenous, Black, and people of color and girls in elective and advanced math and science classes

- Giving students less responsibility (such as managing supplies, using the restroom independently during class, and self-assessment) than they had when they were younger

- Telling students that if they work hard in school and get a good night's sleep and eat a healthy breakfast they will do well on state standardized tests when in your state you know the test has been known to be biased to people of color, emergent bilingual students, and students who come from lower-income households.

Figure 6–4 **Teaching Thomassons for Reflection**

The list in Figure 6–4 is not complete. You'll be able to find more teaching Thomassons if you can start making it a habit. If you're interested in doing some more self-reflection, consider incorporating some cognitive restructuring around negative emotions in your day-to-day teaching.

Be Vigilant: Challenge the Feel-Good Thomassons

Negative emotions can be the most useful guide to spotting Thomassons but they don't always get us there. Sometimes it's the stuff we feel smugly good about that hides the problematic belief. Behaviors that engage a superficial level of thinking but that make us feel cozy, like decorating our room so that it looks Pinterest perfect without student participation, or overscaffolding children so that assignments get done at the level we expect but students don't own any of the thinking because we've done it for them. We feel good about the accomplishment, but the purpose of our activity is obscured and lost. One such feel-good Thomasson I recently tackled for myself is food drives. Twice a year, many schools run donation drives for food, coats, or books. I always felt these initiatives helped students learn real-world service and generosity and also reminded some of the privilege they took for granted. Everyone felt a little bit better about themselves and the world when they participated. And yet one day my longtime friend Cheryl Tyler's brow furrowed in disappointment as I celebrated the latest kindness initiative.

A former classroom teacher, retired principal, and now reading specialist and community activist, Cheryl is one of the more generous, thoughtful people I know. I thought for sure she would be Team Can Drive. And I said as much. "I just think they're a mistake," she said. "Canned food drives and coat drives are a mistake because they create a sense of 'those people' who need coats and food." I could understand the problematic othering she was referring to but had never really thought about its ramifications for children, let alone the othering it would do for students in class who might be currently experiencing a lack of resources. Then she added, "It's our work to teach students about the larger systemic factors that put people in a position where they need food and clothing and how we can dismantle those systems and replace them with structures for economic justice."

In a split second, through Cheryl's words, I saw how pervasive feel-good Thomassons are. I felt good and right when I collected cans for a can drive. I felt good and right when I asked students to do so.

After talking with Cheryl, I understood she wasn't anti–food drives. After all, people do need to eat. But without study, discussion, and actions designed to dismantle the systems that have created a situation where approximately one in seven children live in food insecure homes in the United States, the food drives give people a false sense of making a significant difference, which assuages guilt without solving the problem. When we feel better about something, we are less likely to look at making structural changes. Additionally, by focusing on the people who receive the food, as opposed to the system that causes the hunger, it shifts the burden of responsibility to the hungry and not to our entire community.

If we are willing to look at all of our practices, even our most sacred and dear, seemingly perfect practices, with a clear eye that questions not just how we feel when do them but the purpose they serve for children, we might discover that often the most egregious Thomassons lay in our most beloved actions. And with this knowledge we can make powerful corrections.

SOMETIMES IT'S THE STUFF WE FEEL SMUGLY GOOD ABOUT THAT HIDES THE PROBLEMATIC BELIEF.

A MISTAKE-WELCOMING CLASSROOM CULTURE

The Balance of Belief and Doubt

Writing teacher Peter Elbow worked hard to liberate student writers from the fear of mistake-making. He connected that fear with a traditional Western education's overemphasis on doubt: "You hear an idea and you critique it. You try to find its weaknesses" (Broad, quoted in Hatch 2018). Elbow wasn't questioning the value of skepticism. Of course, he wanted students to be critical thinkers, to question authority, and to use evidence to imagine better solutions. But Elbow felt that doubt needed to be in balance with belief. He explained:

We need to build a richer culture of rationality—richer than mere doubting or critical thinking—so that people will feel that they are not thinking carefully unless they try to believe ideas they don't want to believe . . . If we try systematically to doubt everything, we're not trying to reject everything, we're trying to find flaws we couldn't see before and see which ideas look best after this scrutiny of doubt. If we try systematically to believe everything, we're not trying to accept everything, we're trying to find virtues we couldn't see before and see which ideas look best after this scrutiny of believing. (Broad, quoted in Hatch 2018)

In too many classrooms today, doubt alone exists. If all we teach is doubt, then we foster a binary, all-or-nothing perspective that makes learning a process of fear, one of being caught for not knowing. But when we sit with an idea, even if we know it's mistaken, and consider what might be true about it, what happens? What is possible if it were true? We can get to new, deeper understandings that critique alone can't yield. No matter how cynical we think we are, we are all capable of this kind of thinking. Every time we watch an action/sci-fi/fantasy film or read a novel, we are actively suspending our disbelief. We know that a dragon being ridden across the sky toward the battle isn't real, but for the next thirty seconds we can pretend that it is to enjoy the scene.

The best teachers I've had were ones who could hold belief and doubt together. They could hold their understanding of a concept with my approximation and see my approximation not just for what it lacked but for what it held. They understood why I made certain mistakes because they were able to use their imagination and intellect to follow my sequence of thinking. And they didn't view that thinking as deficit laden but as being informed by an intelligence, a valuable kind of sensemaking that even if inaccurate was reaching for accuracy.

Those of us who have had the privilege of spending time with very young children know how compelling our conversations with them can be. There's often a wisdom, an insight, that our "correct" understandings have overlooked or minimized and that they bring fresh attention to in a way that enriches our own "expert" adult understanding. The wisest psychologists, psychiatrists (particularly those of children like Vygotsky, González, Amanti, Moll, and Rogoff), and anthropologists have used this kind of thinking to understand the experiences of people different from them. They asked, "What would be necessary to make this so?" This balance of belief and doubt shouldn't be reserved for the best thinkers among us; it should be an active part of every student's learning. Not just "What's wrong with this way of solving the problem?" but also "What's right about this way of solving the problem?" This immediately shifts the conversation from who's right and who's wrong to what we can learn from each other.

After talking to countless teachers, I've come to believe specific things in our practice creates a pseudoacceptance culture for mistakes. First and foremost, our assessment systems reward students for mastery over skills and material, not for their work toward learning. If rubrics are created, grades recorded, awards given on mastery, the occasional pep talk or bit of feedback we give about the value of learning through risk-taking and error making feels a bit false. Yes, it is true that many of us have effort, process, and risk-taking on our rubrics and report cards. But, on the whole, the student who makes the least errors gets the top score.

Whether or not we consistently tell our students that learning is what matters and grades don't, students still see that number at the top of the test or the bottom of the rubric or that letter on their report card. As long as final scores are a thing in our classrooms, a growth mindset with an embrace of errors is going to be an uphill battle. Teachers who have decided to teach without grading report that it not only changes the spirit of students in their classes, but it also deeply affects the way they teach. Both teacher and student become more focused on the real goal—learning—rather than the pseudogoal—reported achievement. In her revelatory book *Hack Assessment: 10 Ways to Go Gradeless in a Traditional Grades School,* Starr Sackstein (2015) describes what happened after she ended traditional grading in her high school classroom: "As we rid ourselves of the grades, risk taking and questioning became a natural part of the process."

As Cornelius Minor (2019) explains in *We Got This,* systems we take for granted as "just the way things are" can actually be studied and changed or even dismantled if we discover that they are getting in the way of kids' learning. Minor is speaking not just of our systems of assessment but about how those systems perpetuate societal systems of oppression. For many students, schools are their first and most regular contact with non-familial authority, and for public school students, government structures. Part of what schools do is teach students how power structures and systems work and how they need to behave to be accepted by the larger community within that system or structure. In many school settings students are rewarded or punished for their compliance to a list of expectations. They are expected to conform to the system; the system is only curious about them to the degree they conform or defy. From how they walk in the halls to whether they get access to more or less rigorous learning, compliance defines most children's identities in school and sets their expectations of how they will live in the larger world. Students' learning culture is built one decision at a time by us: moment to moment are we choosing a culture that values learning from mistakes or compliance? Decisions come at us fast and furious but self-monitoring and reflection allow us to recognize how often we're choosing compliance and quiet over agency and voice. Often, these decisions can feel like "givens," which is why we need to keep asking ourselves, is this expectation I have for my students increasing their agency and voice or diminishing it? Am I telling students how to respond or offering them choices? Am I inviting them to imagine something better or limiting possibility? One way of evaluating our classroom learning culture is to consider to what degree we'd characterize our time with students as a conversation versus a list of assignments and commands.

I know not everyone reading this is going to feel ready or even willing to reconsider, let alone dismantle all of the systems that might be obstacles to building a healthy risk-taking and mistake-welcoming culture in their building, such as their current systems of assessment and grading. However, I do think it's worth considering the role those systems play as obstacles for student growth. The stakes are larger than sophomore algebra. We need to create learning cultures. A true learning culture allows us to recognize and learn from not only our own mistakes but the mistakes that exist in the larger culture and that hold all its members back from reaching their full potential. When we model how expert learners learn from mistakes, we show that process as an essential part of participating in the world. We know how much people's refusal to address mistakes leads to the continued suffering of others. Think of how some nations have taken responsibility or not for their founding on the oppression of others (Australia's "Uluru Statement from the Heart" [2017] and Canada's report "Reclaiming Power and Place" [Canadian Observatory of Homelessness 2019] being two recent examples). Compare that to the work that some have done to project the responsibility for their mistakes onto others. Educators can explicitly discuss the ways that acknowledging and addressing mistakes can be gifts for and from even the most expert among us.

To do this work, we need to look closely at ourselves first. See Figure 7-1 for examples of questions of critique and belief.

Teacher Reflection Questions That Balance Critique and Belief

Critical-Minded Questions	Belief-Based Questions
In what ways do I perpetuate systems that value and emphasize perfection and conformity over risk-taking and growth?	What capabilities do children bring to school that are more than/different from what I might be offering or expecting from them?
Are there areas where I have less patience and understanding for mistakes?	When can students teach me?
Am I willing to be more transparent in my own mistake-making so that students are able to see a model of mistake expectation learning?	How can I invite students to challenge my assumptions about what they know and what they need to learn in constructive ways?

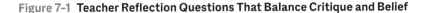

Figure 7-1 **Teacher Reflection Questions That Balance Critique and Belief**

You might have noticed that my critique questions are focused on my practice and the belief questions center on students. Although it's equally important to ask belief questions of ourselves, I've found teachers shift most quickly when we ask belief questions about our students. If it's possible to raise these questions with a colleague or a group of colleagues, you will likely find yourself involved in rather juicy conversations that will lead you to some new ideas.

You might start this work with a look at a standard lesson that you teach. Not your bells and whistle lesson, but one you have taught before and teach regularly. Let's imagine doing this with grammar. Compare the two lessons using the questions I just provided.

Lesson 1: Traditional, Teacher-Centered Lesson on Paragraphs

Aim: Students will learn that paragraphs are used to organize their writing and make it easier to understand for readers.

Lesson steps:

1. Teacher begins by asking students to talk about what they know already about paragraphs.

2. Teacher then gives a definition about paragraphs, incorporating some of the students' responses when appropriate. *A section of writing focused on an idea or moment. Usually indicated by an indent or double-spacing.*

3. Teacher projects a familiar text that is a nice example of paragraphing. Teacher asks students to comment or annotate on what they notice about the author's paragraphing.

4. Teacher shares another text, this time with the paragraphing removed so that the text is entirely in a block. Teacher asks students to work with a partner to share ways to section this text into paragraphs.

5. Students share their choices. Teacher projects and discusses a few exemplars with the class.

6. Teachers asks students to hold paragraphs in mind in their writing today.

This is not a bad lesson. But it is firmly grounded in the notions of convention and compliance. Many people might argue that grammar must be taught that way, precisely because of its emphasis on convention. But, if I wanted to teach the same concept of paragraphing, but with a more belief-based angle, I would instead consider what students come to the class knowing and what language cultures, traditions, and texts they might bring to paragraphing. They also might not know that their knowledge is rich and worthwhile and be less likely to challenge me when I teach grammar because of that, so I will want to put extra emphasis on thinking of ways to ensure students can challenge me. A belief-based lesson, grounded in the idea of embracing mistake-making as part of learning culture, might look something like this:

Lesson 2: Inquiry Lesson into Paragraphs

Aim: Students will build off what they already know or believe about paragraphs in order to challenge their own false and real understandings of them, in order to prune false understandings, retain correct ones, and incorporate new.

Lesson steps:

1. Teacher confesses that there are a lot of myths about paragraphs—probably more myths about paragraphs than almost any other grammatical concept.

2. Teacher asks students to jot what they think they know about paragraphs on sticky notes, placing the notes in columns on a large piece of butcher paper with headings *Know for Sure, Not Sure*, and *Suspected Myth*.

3. Teacher explains that they are very much still learning about the complexities of paragraphs, in part because standard paragraphs have changed so much over the years.

4. Teacher poses an inquiry: Can they choose one of the things they included on the chart and work to discover if it is a truth about paragraphs or a myth or perhaps something in between? Students are encouraged to look in books, magazines, online, and environmental print to find answers.

5. Students scatter throughout the classroom in partnerships, in groups, or solo, gathering evidence. Teacher acts as coach and guide, making suggestions of places to look, raising questions, and asking students to explain their current working theories.

6. Class reconvenes to share. Teacher begins by owning at least one big paragraph myth that was shattered, such as "All paragraphs have a topic sentence" or "Paragraphs must have at least five sentences." And students share their own shattered myths, confirmations, and new learning.

Teacher and students share how many writing choices they've made over the years based off mistaken beliefs about what paragraphs should and should not have. See Figure 7-2 for an example of this inquiry.

In both lessons, students are learning about and exploring paragraphs. Both lessons have fine content. But in the first lesson is an implied assumption that the students know nothing about paragraphs and the teacher knows all. Because of this, whether intended or not, there are limitations to what a paragraph can include—even if it's just due to time and attention spans. In the second lesson, there's an assumption that everyone, including the teachers, is on a learning journey. And the teacher is excited to learn alongside and from the students. For example, some will be shocked to learn that there can be paragraphs that are a sentence long—even a word long! Some will be gobsmacked to discover writers don't actually have to start a new paragraph every time a new speaker speaks. Many authors don't do that. For younger students, the realization that not all paragraphs have a topic sentence is almost equivalent to heresy.

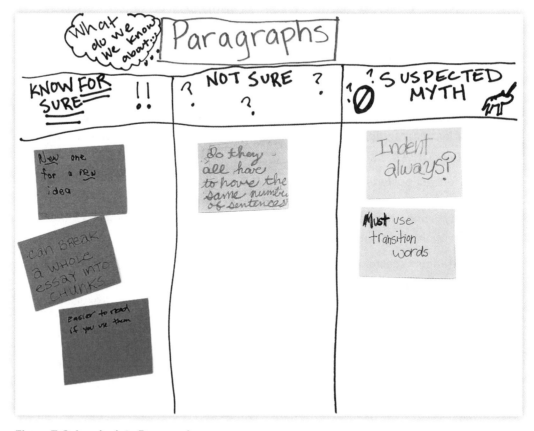

Figure 7-2 Inquiry into Paragraphs

Paragraphs are actually fraught with controversies and mythologies around what they must contain or never do. If you don't believe me, go ahead and jump into a writer's forum online to explore whether professional journalists prefer indented paragraphs or block style. Listen to novelists debate how long a paragraph can be before there's a paragraph break. How does one decide if it's a new paragraph, a period, or a double space break? The varied takes on paragraphing you hear from writers across a range of genres will be fascinating and passionate and exposes just how wide open the world of paragraphs is. By opening those discussions and inquiries to students and letting them in on the secret that there is actually a whole lot of thinking on this topic, you are showing your own curiosity as well as willingness to not be the expert. Looking through trade magazines and social media groups for professional writers and reading a range of grammar and convention books such as *The Dash of Style* by Noah Lukeman (2007), *The Deluxe Transitive Vampire* (Gordon 1993), or the classic *Elements of Style* by Strunk and White (1999), it will become abundantly clear that nothing is cut-and-dried in the world of grammar, and even the most seasoned grammarian has new tricks to learn. Grammar contains multitudes, as do teachers. (As is true of any discipline.) This lesson shares these insights with students. In both instances the students are learning about paragraphs, but in the second one, students are also learning the messy, imperfect, exciting act of learning.

Making Mistakes Part of Our Curriculum

We need to consciously think through how our day-to-day interactions with students, our classrooms' environment, and our curriculum consciously support the mistake mindset we value. We should be planful, with arms full of materials, ideas, and activities to help give form and vision to the countless teachable moments we experience on a daily basis. And just as we would pore through lessons, create unit goals, and develop experiences and assessments for our so-called hard skill instruction, it's just as important for us to be as mindful in our creation of a learning culture for mistakes in our classrooms and buildings. We can do this in countless ways, big and small. We might begin by considering materials in our classroom, rituals we create, and our own demonstration of mistake-making and response. See Figure 7–3 for some ideas.

Grammar contains multitudes, as do teachers. (As is true of any discipline.)

&

Euclid's proof that all Δ's are isoceles – inaccurate drawing

silly putty

Michael Jordan

"I have missed more than 9000 shots in my career. I've lost almost 300 games. 26 times, I've been trusted to take the game winning shot + missed. I've failed over + over again in my life, + that is why I succeed."

Opportunity	Instruction
Behavioral mistakes	Instead of following standard punitive models, consider implementing an inquiry model into mistakes both for yourself and your students. What really happened and why? How can we make this better? How do we use restorative circles or another impact focused, rather than punitive, framework? (See page 51 for resources.) We can support this work by also exploring other people's full humanity as artists, politicians, scientists, mathematicians.
Historical figures/ decision-making in math, science, social studies	Identify the mistakes that historical figures have made that could have been prevented, that were informed by key misunderstandings, and/or that led to greater understandings. The central thread of this study should be that having the integrity to examine one's mistakes leads to the greater welfare of all. Know that this is an opportunity to address socioemotional knowledge, too. Gaps in public figures' socioemotional knowledge are often the source of mistakes. Too often, historical figures are canonized as "heroes," with little acknowledgment of their complicated natures, or they're dismissed as "geniuses but . . ." It is common for people to want to idolize or tear down (again, a false binary) but neither gives us useful or particularly truthful information for students or the culture at large. Instead of summing up public figures for students based on someone else's opinion ("He was a product of his times"), students can inquire into what their success meant in the larger society, what they struggled with to be successful, how they were able or not to hold on to positive values, and what that meant for the work they were celebrated for.
Process share in all content areas	Make mistake-sharing an essential part of all process work shares. After a problem-solve, book club, science experiment, social studies research project, ask students, "Who made a useful mistake?" and make sharing the mistake a positive experience. The purpose of the sharing is to lead to better learning—improved work processes, further clarified conceptual understandings. Pay attention to the language you and your students use to describe mistakes, making certain to gently correct any excessively negative language.
Read-aloud	Pick books (see list in Figure 7–4) that show fictional characters and real people not feeling/overcoming shame from their mistakes and learning from them.
Teacher modeling, all content areas	Include some mistakes that you have made in your evolving understanding of the content area that you think students might encounter. Set up situations where you tell students that you are going to make a mistake on purpose and encourage your students to catch your mistake.

Opportunity	Instruction
Inquiry, all content areas	Share mistake-making that asks students to identify and evaluate other people's mistakes. In language arts, ask students to improve a problematic piece of writing for language and content. In social studies and science, share the data that informed a historical figure's decision and any additional useful data and ask students to identify the mistaken decision-making. One classic example from science: Adolphe Quetelet's invention of the concept of "normal" (Rose 2016). In mathematics or science, show how one mathematician/scientist built on the work of another and ask students to identify the clarified and corrected understandings made over time.

Figure 7-3 **Opportunities for Teaching Around Mistakes**

THE VALUE OF (SOME) INTENTIONAL MISTAKES

There is something to be said about mistakes intentionally made. I first read about intentionally made mistakes by a professional in, of all places, a book about magic, *Win the Crowd: Unlock the Secrets of Influence, Charisma and Showmanship* by Steve Cohen (2009). He is known as "The Millionaire's Magician" because he regularly performs in private shows for the very rich. He had a long-running show in the presidential suite in the Waldorf Astoria in New York City, which is where I saw him. His magic specialty is small magic—sleights of hand, card tricks, and the like. Stuff you need to be up close to see. More intimate magic than the big illusions we have gotten used to seeing in televised spectacles. A lot of magicians, such as Penn and Teller, say this style of intimate magic is the most difficult to be good at because it is much harder to hide your tricks when your audience is inches away. Steve Cohen is one of the top performers of this sort of magic. For hours and days after seeing one of his shows, I would find myself wondering how he did this trick or that.

So you can imagine my surprise when as I was reading his book and I discovered that he intentionally makes at least one big mistake toward the beginning of his show. "One of the techniques magicians use is Planned Failure. I greatly enjoy planning out my failures—in fact, I rehearse them. I believe that people want to see other people fail. And they want to see those people overcome failure. The bigger that failure, the greater the impact when the desired income actually occurs" (Cohen 2009, 79-80). He does this for a few reasons. One reason is that when a magician makes a mistake at the beginning of the show, it's a great way to break the ice. Everyone knows that certain people are not supposed to make mistakes: brain surgeons, professional athletes, magicians, and, of course, teachers. So when the audience first starts watching the show, they are all nerves. What if he makes a mistake? But, once the mistake is made, the supposedly worst has happened, and we can relax.

The mistakes work because there is also way in which audiences are sort of rooting against the magician. After all, the whole conceit is that the magician is here to fool you. And although none of us like to appear foolish, we did all show up to this show to be fooled. But, more often than not, we like to think we will not be fooled. That we will be able to figure out every trick. We don't like the idea of the magician having more power than we do. So, yes, we are rooting against the magician totally fooling us. We are watching with an eagle eye. But, when or if the magician makes a mistake, we find ourselves immediately more sympathetic. "Yikes. That's bad luck. But he handled that well. So I'm pulling for him." And consciously or not we soften our eagle eye and give ourselves permission to be fooled, almost as a way to support the slightly disgraced performer. This reminds me very much of how it is to be a teacher almost everywhere. We are the experts and there's a way in which our students, especially, look to us to be perfect. When we walk through our classrooms, whether teaching our lessons, coaching our students, or writing chatty newsletters to families, we are viewed as the experts. And although many of our students, especially if we teach young ones, view us as almost perfect, they and their families are very much like the audience in a magic show. They are eagle-eyed for mistakes, misinformation, misspellings, miscalculations, missteps. If you've been teaching for longer than five minutes, you've experienced the joyous glee from a student pointing out one of your errors or a grown-up conspiratorially "letting you know" about an error they caught.

Steve Cohen explains that making an early and obvious mistake *on purpose* actually increases belief among the entire audience—both believers and nonbelievers. This is a curious idea that I have come to adopt in my own practice. Because, yes, <u>mistakes make us</u> <u>more human for our students</u>. But I have also seen that just like the audience in a magic show, students are more likely to soften their gaze and root for us, more likely to believe in us when we make that mistake.

Sometimes the mistake is not intentional. But I have gotten into the habit that if something hasn't gone wrong accidentally by the first five minutes in my teaching, I intentionally make a mistake. Sometimes the mistake is something physical, like dropping a marker or having trouble connecting the projector. Other times it's something students spot right away, like misspelling a common word or forgetting to do some procedure I nag them about all the time.

Still other times, especially when I feel like the work I am teaching is intellectually or emotionally risky, I make a mistake that models exactly the kind of mistake they are likely to be concerned about making. This could be about taking a risk with a conclusion drawn, a choice in algorithms to use, an interpretation of data, a play to run on the soccer field. When we do this, we break the ice, for sure, but we also remove the stigma surrounding those types of mistakes. If a teacher can make this type of mistake, students glean, surely anyone can. Additionally, when I make that mistake, I also have an opportunity to model how ones goes about reacting to and rebounding from that mistake. Some might argue that this kind of planned mistake-making can disrupt students' trust of us. If students recognize the manipulation, then they can feel distrustful of us. That's certainly important to keep in mind. What really matters is the spirit we do this work in. If we're focusing on tricking the students, they will see through that to some degree, but if we're <u>focused on helping them see that no one is perfect</u>, we are imperfect, then the intentional mistake-making increases the emotional safety in our classroom.

When we make an honest mistake (or a planned one), it is a wonderful time to model ways we can deal well with mistakes, not just how we respond to fixing the mistake but to how we react when other people point out our mistakes and even how to point out other people's mistakes in constructive ways. We can even model unproductive ways of responding to mistakes (in ways that keep children feeling safe), like responding to a student's correction by saying something like, "Now, if I felt that a mistake meant that I was worth less as a person, I might throw down my eraser and say, 'I've had enough! I'm not going to do this anymore!' but if I understood that mistakes are part of the process, I might instead say, 'Give me a second. I'm not sure what I did wrong. Can you explain that to me again?'" Think about it—never are students more focused on us as when we make a mistake. All eyes are on us, with rapt attention. We shouldn't overlook that kind of engagement.

Despite that fact that in my professional life I know I learn best from experts who also share their own stories of imperfection, I sometimes get a lump in my throat, or need to take a deep breath before I . . . admit . . . expose . . . confess . . . It's even difficult to find the right verb to use right before the word *mistake* to describe sharing one. I attribute this difficulty to the heavy freight that our society attaches to mistakes, but I also believe that regular and specific conversations and instruction is also bound to be helpful in destigmatizing mistakes. Recently, because of the popularity of the work of Brené Brown, Sheila Heen, and others, there is a lot of talk about the role vulnerability plays in our relationships, as well as our roles, especially as leaders. Often the idea of vulnerability is translated to mean sharing our feelings as leaders. However, sharing our stories of foibles and miscalculations, as well as the aftermath, can go a long way toward making that same vulnerability not only acceptable but also welcomed into our learning communities.

When considering the best ways to demonstrate mistake response to your students, you might want to first consider the ways your students already respond to mistakes. Especially the ways you think can be improved upon. Do they beat themselves up? Pretend it didn't happen? Give up? Whatever they tend to do, you might want to start there and then move on to "catching yourself" and instead going for something better—something you wish they would do.

So this might look something like this:

```
INT. CLASSROOM (TEACHING)

TEACHER standing at front of the room, demonstrating equation.
Close-up on clear mathematical error.

                    TEACHER
          Oh shoot! I totally messed this one up. I'm super
          tempted to just scribble this out and make an
          excuse for why I did this part wrong.

STUDENTS exchange looks and murmur among themselves. TEACHER
takes visible deep breath. Appears to be thinking something over.

                    TEACHER
          But this is all on me. And I know I made this
          mistake because I was sort of taking it for
          granted that I knew how this equation was going
          to end up. So instead, I'm going to remind myself
          never to take something for granted—even if it
          appears easy—especially if it appears easy. When
          something is hard, I tend to be more careful,
          but I was really phoning that one in. Let me try
          this again.

TEACHER returns to solving equation.
```

When deciding to go this route, some steps we might consider taking to maximize learning potential include:

1. When teaching something you know has many opportunities for mistakes, stay wide awake for either your own errors or for opportunities to demonstrate errors.

2. If possible, choose to explicitly model a "not" example first, chosen because of your students' tendency to respond to errors in similar ways.

3. Model opting out of going with that unproductive model.

As you plan your modeling of intentional mistakes, it might be worth reflecting for a bit on the language you and your students use around errors. Do some students hear some errors described in one way and some in another way? Do some errors receive different language than others? It is interesting to notice that there is a hierarchy in terms of the ways we value or worry about error. Most of us are not concerned by a small slipup or flub, but we are more concerned about a miscalculation and even more concerned about damage.

When talking about mistakes to students, the tone that we take, the adjectives that we use, the context we refer to, can make all the difference. Although we don't want to use infantilizing language that minimizes mistakes, we also want to avoid language that makes mistake-making seem like an all-or-nothing risky scenario. When students are trying out a new skill or discussing a new concept and we speak in terms of *understandable* or *expected* mistakes, that sends a very different message than when we talk about *careless* or *lazy* mistakes. Even when, for all intents and purposes, the mistake is quantifiably the same one, the way we contextualize the mistake has a lot of power in deciding whether the student will learn from that mistake and keep going or whether they will give up.

TEXTS ARE OUR CO-TEACHERS

So much of our work with our students about mistakes is going to feel personal in nature. At times we're going to feel like all we do is talk about our own mistakes and encourage students to do the same. However, it is also important that students learn from others—both from narratives designed to teach and nonfiction based on research. My guess is that you likely already have a few texts about mistakes in your collection that you can guide students to read or use in lessons. However, you might not have yet organized them in a purposeful way. If that is the case for you, creating a spot in your classroom for a curated collection of books, articles, or multimodal texts that touch upon mistakes and related topics can be a strong foundation to build your mistakes-based instruction upon. See Figure 7–4 for a few suggestions organized by grade range. Please note, this is a rough grouping and there are possibilities that might be appropriate for any age found across the grade ranges. It is also important to preview each item to determine if it is right for your students.

MISTAKES MAKE US MORE HUMAN FOR OUR STUDENTS.

Texts That Teach About Mistake-Making

	Primary	Middle Grade	Middle School	High School
Books	*The Book of Mistakes* by Corinna Luyken (2017) *Beautiful Oops* by Barney Saltzberg (2010) *Even Superheroes Make Mistakes* by Shelly Becker (2018)	*Mistakes That Worked* by Charlotte Foltz Jones (2016) *How to Take the Ache Out of Mistakes* by Kimberly Feltes Taylor and Eric Braun (2019) *What to Do When Mistakes Make You Quake* by Clare Freeland and Jacqueline Toner (2015)	*Disaster Strikes! The Most Dangerous Space Missions of All Time* by Jeffrey Kluger (2019) *Imperfect: Poems About Mistakes—An Anthology for Middle Schoolers*, edited by Tabatha Yeatts (2018)	*Is It Still Cheating If I Don't Get Caught?* by Bruce Weinstein (2009)
Articles		"Noticing Mistakes Boosts Learning" (Stevens 2019) (see Bibliography)	"Six Beautiful Mistakes Caught on Camera" (Wender 2015) (see Bibliography)	"So You've Made a Huge Mistake. Now What?" (Herrera 2019b) (see Bibliography)
Multimedia	"Talks About Making Mistakes" (an episode of *Mr. Rogers' Neighborhood*) (PBS Kids 1987) (see Bibliography)	"Learning from Design 'Mistakes'" (ABC Education 2011) (see Bibliography)	"My Favorite No" (Midwinter 2015) (see Bibliography)	"Patti LaBelle: 'Where Are My Background Singers?'" (Bloomquist 2016) (see Bibliography)

Figure 7–4 Texts That Teach About Mistake-Making

FAILURE AND REFLECTION

Creating habits and rituals in our classrooms helps demystify and normalize the things we value. We do this across our days when students grow to expect that every day or almost every day we do (fill in the blank with something your students experience in your classroom). Whether it's quick math fact practice, hot topic discussion groups, or a close read of a historical document, when it comes to academic work, the more it is woven into our days the more fluency our students develop with that content or skill. This is, not surprisingly, also true of our work around teaching mistakes. We can create a habit or ritual in the classroom around mistakes to welcome failure through mistakes boxes. I most often use this activity in grades K–3. (For a slightly different take on this for older students, grades 4–12, see "Mistakes Résumé" in lesson 6.)

To introduce mistakes boxes, I gather the students and say, "I once read an article by an expert on failure who talked about the value of having a failure box. The idea is that when we fail, we tend to do one of two things—either try to forget about it as quickly as possible or do almost the opposite and perseverate on it. But, the idea of the failure box is that, instead of doing that, we can write down our failures when we have them, on a little piece of paper or a card, and place them in a box. That way we can both acknowledge them but also let them go. And then at another point we can look back through the failures in that box and look to see what kind of story they tell. It sort of reminds me of a friend of mine who, when she got her first book published, decorated the party with all her rejection letters. Yes, the new book was to be celebrated, but also, so was the whole journey."

I then go on to explain that although mistakes and failures are not exactly the same, there can be overlap. Like, you can have a failure and not have made a single mistake—for example, you might play the best game of your life, error free, and still have lost because the other side got lucky or maybe were just even better. But on the flip side, you can make mistakes left and right and still not fail. "But I think a lot of us agree that mistakes and failure are related," I say. I then hold up my own mistakes box. "I was thinking, maybe we can borrow a move from the failure world? Maybe we could create mistakes boxes. And when we make a mistake, just like with failure boxes, instead of either trying to forget about it or think about it too much, we can spend a minute writing it down and then placing it in the box. Then later, when we feel like we want to maybe study a pattern or perhaps see how much we've grown, we can open up those boxes."

At this point I show a few mistakes I have collected in my own box. Depending on the kind of teacher you are, the box can be as artistic or as plain as you like. In my case it is an old tissue box I had painted. I pull out a few pieces of paper with mistakes written upon them I had previously shared with the class and a few new ones. "You know looking at these, there are a few feelings I'm having. On the one hand, I still feel a tingle of embarrassment from these mistakes. But on the other hand, there is something kind of great about knowing I have moved past these. I am already not doing these things anymore, or at least doing these less. If I feel like one is not getting any better, and I wish it were, I might want to take a couple of minutes to reflect on that, or I might want to talk to a friend about it. The most important thing about this isn't that I spend all this time collecting these mistakes to feel bad about them, but rather so that I can help myself notice patterns and notice when and how I grow." See Figure 7-5 for some examples from students.

- Mispronounced a student's name

- Left my coffee on the kitchen counter

- Began teaching the wrong lesson because my plans were open to the wrong day

After sharing my own mistakes box, I then give students the opportunity to make their own and a place to store them in the classroom. Depending on the age and maturity of your students and whether or not they share the space with other students, you might want to have a designated spot for students to keep their boxes that is both easy to access but also makes it unlikely students will be able to read each other's mistakes without permission.

Keeping easy to grab pieces of paper, whether just cut pieces of scratch paper or index cards, available near the boxes so that kids can easily jot down a mistake whenever they want can also make it more likely this becomes a habit in your classroom. After the initial

Figure 7-5 Student Mistake Papers (K-3)

introduction and creation, some teachers might create a regular time to jot mistakes down for the day or week. Others might want to create a weekly reflection time where students take out their boxes and look through mistakes they've made and any thoughts they have about them.

Of course, our modeling of noting and reflecting regularly on the mistakes box is perhaps the most important part of this. The more we are able to regularly model acknowledging our mistakes, perhaps often jotting them down or taking the time to pull out the box and reflect, the more students will find this whole process something that not only young learners do, but those of us who are further down the journey as well.

The Space We Hold Is the Space Students Grow Into

Recently, while in quarantine for COVID-19, I found myself down a rabbit hole of myths and discovered that something I had always believed was true was not only false, but also harmful. I learned, much to my surprise, that goldfish do not somehow magically limit their growth to the bowl size they have. The myth started because people noticed their goldfish would grow and grow and then stop. And then, not too long after, they would die. Which led people to believe that was a goldfish's natural lifespan. But, actually, goldfish can grow pretty large (to slightly over a foot) and live for pretty long (for over a decade). When or if they outgrow their environment, they die. If they can't outgrow their environment, they will live and grow for a very long time. Many, many goldfish die too soon because their caregivers wrongly believe that their goldfish would stop growing without harm in whatever size environment they chose to provide.

I see a connection between how goldfishes' life span has been artificially truncated by their human companions and how students' learning can be limited by teachers choosing not to make classrooms safe for mistake-making. Everyone believes they are making enough space for students to grow, but what we see as the natural limitations of our students and their abilities might have less to do with their innate abilities and more to do with the environment we are building for and with them.

We need to model with our own mistake-making, study and improve our own responses to others' mistakes, adjust our mistake-supporting and -denying habits, and create systems and structures that explicitly teach and prioritize error-making and failure-rich learning. As I move more and more fully into this brave new world of taking more ownership for the mistakes students make when under my care, or their unwillingness to make those mistakes, I find it helpful to look to inspiration to help me get past my anxiety. I find this quote from Carl Jung (1973) inspirational: "Mistakes are, after all, the foundations of truth."

Lesson 1

UNDERSTANDING THE WORD *MISTAKE*

Grades: K–3

Time needed: Approximately 20 minutes

Materials:

- Newsprint or large pieces of drawing or construction paper

- Markers or crayons

- Demonstration chart or whiteboard or display for teacher

Lesson steps:

1. Begin by asking the students to show with a nod or thumb if they have heard the word *mistake* before.

2. Explain that lots of people use that word, but they don't always mean the same thing.

3. On a piece of chart paper or other display, record your definition for the word *mistake*. I might record something like this: "*Mistake*: when you try to do something, but it turns out differently than you meant because of something you did" because I feel

like it's clearer than other definitions and more connected to the mistakes made when learning. You might say something like, "There are different dictionary definitions or even community definitions. But for our purposes as students in this classroom, I'm going to use this definition."

4. Draw a T-chart underneath your definition and write on one side *Mistake* and on the other *Not Mistake*.

5. Sketch one quick example of a mistake (spilling water, forgetting your coat) and one quick example of a "not mistake" (pushing someone, choosing to ignore the teacher).

6. Ask the students to work with a partner or a small group to brainstorm their own examples of actions that are mistakes and actions that are not mistakes (based on intention), and record on the newsprint or large pieces of drawing paper.

7. Remind students that they can use drawing or words to express their ideas. Coach in as needed.

8. Give the students 5–10 minutes to work.

9. Ask students to share with another partnership or group.

10. Display students' work, talking through some of their ideas.

Lesson 2

DEFINING THE WORD *MISTAKE*

Grades: 4-12

**Time
needed:**   Approximately 30 minutes

Materials:

- Newsprint, large pieces of construction paper, or a way to digitally display group work

- Markers or pens

- Chart paper, whiteboard, or digital display for teacher

Lesson steps:

1. Begin by explaining that this class is going to spend some time over the next few days, weeks, or months talking about mistakes.

2. Share that sometimes talking about mistakes can get confusing because people have different definitions or understandings of what the term *mistake* means.

3. Share your definition of *mistake*, recording it visually, preferably with icons or illustrations. My definition is: "A mistake is an action that goes differently than it was intended or meant to

go." You might add, for transparency purposes: "There are other definitions if you were to look it up, or ask members of our larger community. But for the purposes of this class and the ways we want to study and use mistakes for deeper learning, this is the definition I'm going to use."

4. Ask students to explain to someone next to them how they would define the word *mistake* in their own words. "As you're saying it, explain how your definition is similar to or different than mine."

5. Explain that one of the best ways to truly understand a word or concept is to use the Frayer model. "The Frayer Model was created in 1969 by Dorothy Frayer and other thinkers at the University of Wisconsin. It is great for learning new words and terminology, but it is also great for seeing how much we understand a concept and to help us explain what we know to others." Explain that you think it works best when you do the thinking with a partner or group so you can run ideas past each other. Go over the parts of the Frayer model and perhaps sketch out a blank version.

    a. Word definition

    b. Characteristics

    c. Examples

    d. Not examples

6. Figure L–1 is an example of a filled-in Frayer model to share with students.

7. *Optional:* Show a sample Frayer model using another word, perhaps one from your curriculum such as *fractal, justice, democracy,* or *decimal.*

Definition: A mistake is an action that goes wrong

Characteristics:
- Not on purpose
- Accidental
- Slipup
- Sometimes when trying something hard

Mistake

Examples:
- Texting the wrong person
- Forgetting to do something
- Miscalculating an easy problem

Not examples:
- Pretending to be sick to get out of something
- Plagiarizing

Figure L-1 **Teacher Example of Frayer Model for *Mistake***

8. Ask the students to work with a partner or small group to brainstorm their thinking about mistakes. They can use words, pictures, or symbols. See Figure L–2.

9. If time allows, ask groups to pair up with another group and compare ideas.

Figure L-2 **Student Frayer Model for *Mistake***

Lesson 3

"BUT I DIDN'T MEAN TO!" INTENT VERSUS IMPACT

Grades: K-3

Time needed: 20-30 minutes

Materials:

- A copy of a picture book that discusses the role of a mistake-maker dealing with their impact. I suggest *Even Superheroes Make Mistakes* by Shelly Becker (2018).

- Definitions of the terms *intent* and *impact* or words that feel more accessible to your students but have similar meanings, such as *on purpose/accidental* and *effect*, displayed on chart paper, sentence strips, or large sticky notes.

- *Optional:* Blank paper to make modified versions of social stories about situations where the mistake-maker focuses on impact versus intent. The original idea of a Social Story was created by Carol Gray in 1991 specifically to support students on the autism spectrum with understanding social situations.

Since that time, some teachers have found it helpful to use the concept, if not all of the guidelines, to create stories that help all students learn about social interactions through retold or reimagined events told in illustrated story form, matching the students involved with the concept being taught.

Special notes:

This lesson is designed to help students understand that although intent is important, when studying and trying to make amends for our mistakes, we need to pay more attention to the impact of our actions. For some students, especially students who have either been on the receiving end of mistakes that have caused a lasting impact or caused them, this lesson could be difficult. For this reason this lesson is positioned to be about broad understanding instead of deep introspection. As is the case with all lessons of this nature, students should not feel forced to participate.

Lesson steps:

1. Begin by sharing a simple story where you made a mistake and caused some minor harm, but when you apologized you made a point of saying, "I didn't mean to," as opposed to focusing on the harm you caused. You might say something along the lines of, "The other day I was at the grocery store and I was in a rush when I returned my cart. I was all the way to the sidewalk when I heard a commotion and saw the cart I returned hadn't been pushed in enough and was rolling through the parking lot! I watched a worker who was gathering loose carts have to stop what she was doing and go catch my cart. She saw me watching her. I yelled out, 'Sorry! I thought I pushed it in all the way!' She sort of gave me a dirty look. And at first I was like—wow that's kind of rude. But then I thought about how I didn't really apologize for giving her extra work. I had just let her know I hadn't meant to make the cart roll."

2. Explain that today you're going to look more closely at that. "I want to look back at that time with the store worker and the

cart and think about what I could have done differently with my mistake."

3. Read aloud a picture book that illustrates that point. In this lesson I recommend the book *Even Superheroes Make Mistakes*. It focuses on mistakes superheroes make and then their choice to do what they can to make things right. You might introduce the book by saying something like, "This is a book about how superheroes make mistakes. We might be tempted to just focus on their mistakes, but let's also keep an eye out for what they do to make things right after they make a mistake."

4. Ask students to share with a partner their initial thoughts about the book. "Now that we're done with this book, I'd like you to think about what you noticed about how the superheroes ended up handling their mistakes."

5. Share the definitions of *intent* and *impact* or *meant to* and *effect*.

6. Explain that intent does matter. "When we are hurt, it can feel better when the person who hurt us didn't mean to. That it wasn't on purpose. A lot of us focus on whether we meant to make the mistake when we apologize. That's what I did when I apologized to the worker."

7. Point out that the impact of the effects or consequences of our actions is what we should really try to apologize for and make better if we can. "What also matters a lot, probably even more, is the impact, or how badly we were hurt or how badly we hurt someone else. So, just like the superheroes tried to make things right and focus on that, we can do that too."

8. *Optional:* Ask students to work in partnerships or teams, or perhaps even as a whole class, to create a social story to help illustrate the idea of intent versus impact.

Lesson 4

INTENT VERSUS IMPACT

Grades: 4-12

**Time
needed:**   15-30 minutes, depending whether article is used

Materials:

- *Optional:* An article or video clip discussing the use of the language *crash* versus *accident* such as "It's No Accident. Advocates Want to Speak of Car 'Crashes' Instead" by Matt Richtel (2016)

- Chart paper or other place to record and display conversation

Special notes:

*This lesson is designed to help students understand that although intent is impor-
tant, when studying and trying to make amends for our mistakes, we need to pay
more attention to the impact of our actions. For some students, especially students
who have been on the receiving end of mistakes that have caused a lasting impact,
this lesson could be difficult. For this reason this lesson is positioned to be about
broad understanding instead of deep introspection. As is the case with all lessons
of this nature, students should not feel forced to participate.*

Lesson steps:

1. Begin by telling a story about a time someone made a mistake that caused you harm. For example, a time someone was reading the text messages on their phone, not looking where they were going, and slammed into you, spilling your coffee.

2. Ask students to think, "Which matters more, whether the person who made the mistake meant to slam into me? Or the impact: the fact that I ended up stumbling, spilling my drink, and covering my work in coffee?"

3. Comment that most people would choose the impact as mattering more. "Although it does matter if I intended to do something bad to someone, most of the time that's not the most important thing. So focusing too much on that when I think about my mistake, especially if I'm apologizing, is a little bit of a waste of time. Instead, I need to think of the impact."

4. Display or record the words *impact* and *intent* and their definitions.

Intent	Impact
What we meant to do, purpose	The effects, consequences, or results of an action

5. Share that many of us, when we were small, were taught that the most important thing we could do was apologize. And many of us got into the habit of saying, "I'm sorry. I didn't mean to . . ."

6. Explain that we are now learning that most people do not actually mean to hurt other people, so focusing on intent in everyday life is less important than the effect or impact of our behavior.

7. *Optional:* Read or ask students to read article "It's No Accident: Advocates Want to Speak of Car 'Crashes' Instead" and discuss what this makes them think.

8. Discuss how, as students of mistakes, it is important for us to focus less on our intentions (unless they were bad) and more on the impact—who was harmed or affected by our actions. "If we need to apologize, the apology should spend more time talking about the impact we caused, and if possible any actions we can do to make things better. We can check in with the person or people who were most impacted and see if there is a way to make things right."

Lesson 5

MISTAKES BOX

Grades: K–3

**Time
needed:**   20 minutes for main lesson and box making (Later time should
be set aside for follow-up.)

Materials:

- A tissue box, shoebox, or other small cardboard box for
  each student

- Construction paper, stickers, markers, paint, or other materials
  for decoration

- Small pieces of paper or index cards (several available for each
  student; can be placed in a bin or basket to share or individual
  stacks provided for each student)

- A demonstration mistakes box of your own with prepared
  mistakes you can share with students to model

Special notes:

*This lesson is designed to destigmatize mistake-making while also helping stu-
dents become more metacognitive about their mistakes. However, for some children, this work can be attached to shame. This lesson should be approached with
a lighthearted tone. At no time should a child who does not want to participate be
made to do so.*

Lesson steps:

1. Begin by noting how the class has been talking about mistakes a lot lately. And just like when you've studied other things as a class, it is helpful to spend some time collecting and looking closely at mistakes. "We've been talking a lot about mistakes, just like we've been studying a lot of other things in class, like plants and numbers and letters. And just like we've collected lots of examples of them so we can study them closely, we're going to start collecting mistakes so we can study them more closely."

2. Explain that when we spend time studying something, in this case mistakes, we can look for patterns and characteristics and we can have better discussions about them. "Remember how we looked at parsley and cilantro and noticed how many ways they were similar and how many ways they were different? Well, we can do the same kind of close study of mistakes."

3. Discuss how you thought it would be a good idea to create mistakes boxes for each student as a way to collect and study mistakes when they come up. "Of course, we can't just have our mistakes flying everywhere. So I thought it would be a good idea to have a place for each of us to store our own. Like a mistakes box."

4. Share your mistakes box. Point out how you decorated it and that you look at it as a positive, scientific thing—a way to study mistakes you've made to see if there were ones you could learn more from or ones that follow any patterns.

5. Model thinking of one mistake, jotting it down on a slip of paper, and placing the paper in a box. "I think I'll jot down that fact mistake I made the other day. Remember when I put the entire wrong country down in our social studies lesson? That's

a perfect one." I might say. Ideally this would be a mistake the students know about because it happened in front of them or you've talked about it before.

6. If possible, model talking about another mistake of a different sort. Make sure to talk about how this is a mistake you feel comfortable talking about and that you wouldn't include mistakes that felt vulnerable or you would be embarrassed to discuss.

7. Give students time and materials to decorate their own boxes.

8. For the next few days, keep the boxes close by and regularly model dropping your own mistakes into the box while also reminding and encouraging the students to do the same.

9. After collecting for enough days that students have a small collection, spend some time reflecting on any patterns they see, possibly using other lessons from this section.

Lesson 6

MISTAKES RÉSUMÉ

Grades: 4–12

**Time
needed:**   10–15 minutes

Materials:

- Sample traditional résumé to display

- Sample mistakes résumé you've put together to display

- For your reference: see Tim Herrera's (2019a) "Do You Keep a Failure Résumé? Here's Why You Should Start"

- Materials for students to create their own mistakes résumé

Special notes:

This lesson is designed to destigmatize mistake-making while also helping students become more metacognitive about their mistakes. However, for some children, this work can be attached to shame. This lesson should be approached with a lighthearted tone. At no time should a child who does not want to participate be made to do so.

Lesson steps:

1. Begin by asking students if they know what a résumé is.

2. Show them an example of a traditional résumé and explain that résumés are usually used to help a person get a job by showing

their past experiences. They are a way to politely show off the good things we've done.

3. Explain that although where we went to school and what we did well, such as awards and grades and other accomplishments, are wonderful, it is also interesting to consider the ways in which the mistakes we made led to some of our biggest successes. "We all know that some of the best things that have happened in history were because of a mistake. Our own lives aren't any different."

4. Share your mistakes résumé, talking through how one mistake led to something positive on your résumé. For example, you might show how missing the deadline for one college application led to you going to the college where you fell in love with teaching. Or how because you missed a shot in the big game you ended up not making varsity and trying out for the school play instead. Share those mistakes as bullets under your more traditional elements. This is something you will want to prepare ahead of time so you know which mistakes you're going to talk about, ones you know you feel no shame in sharing.

5. Ask students to try this by starting with a few big achievements then going back and reflecting on any mistakes that influenced those achievements. "I'd like you to try this. You may not have a full résumé because you're not adults. But you have done a lot in your life so far—you've had some big accomplishments and you can base your résumé on those things."

6. Students work on their résumés.

7. Share with a partner or whole group if time.

Lesson 7

TYPES OF MISTAKES

Grades: 2–12

Materials:

- Prepared blank chart that will be filled in during the lesson with the four types of mistakes either on sticky notes or written in

- A video, possibly previously viewed, such as *Snack Attack* (2015) or one that is newer to the students such as *Last Shot* (Widodo 2016)

- Students sitting with partners to talk with

Special notes:

This lesson is adapted from the work of Eduardo Briceño. To read more on his ideas about mistake types see "Mistakes Are Not All Created Equal" in Mindset Works (Briceño 2015a).

Lesson steps:

1. Begin by talking about how there are different types of mistakes. That even though we often talk about how all mistakes have something to teach us, some teach us more than others and some might not be worth the risk if we can avoid them. "If you look at this chart, you can see most mistakes fall on these axes. They go from least purposeful to most. And from least amount of learning that happens because of them to most."

2. Discuss the following mistakes (see Figure L–3), either adding them to the chart or pointing them out as you talk:

a. Sloppy mistakes are mistakes that happen because we just weren't as focused as we could be, we were in a rush, or we could have handled the situation better in another way. These are pretty low-consequence mistakes, and we didn't mean to make them.

b. Aha moment mistakes are mistakes that we learn something by doing them that we didn't know before. This

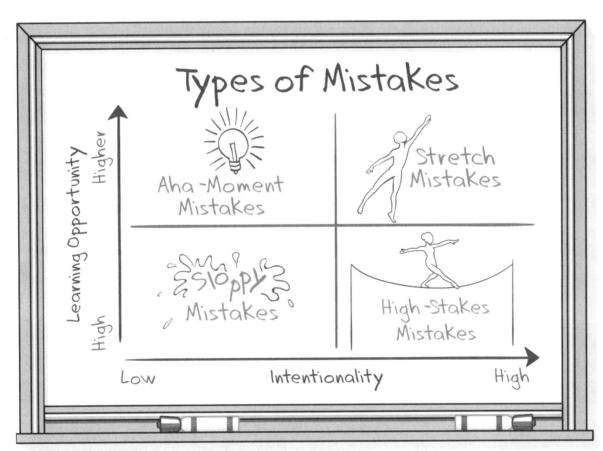

 Source: Mindset Works (www.mindsetworks.com)

Figure L-3 Types of Mistakes

usually happens when our aim is one thing but something unexpected happens along the way so that we learn from that unexpected thing.

c. Stretch mistakes are the best kids of mistakes. We learn a lot from them and we thought we would. They happen when we try something new or just outside our ability so we mess up a bit, but learn a lot.

d. High-stakes mistakes are the worst and we want to avoid them. We know we're doing something hard so we might make a mistake, but the cost of the mistake is very high and often what we learn is not very large or not worth it.

3. If possible, give an example for each kind of mistake from a classroom experience the students would connect with. So, if you're a math teacher, use a math example. Or if you're an elementary teacher, this could involve anything across the disciplines. "The other day when we had a fire drill, remember how I started to head toward the wrong exit door? You all reminded me that we were exiting out a new door now. But we had gotten pretty far down the hall before we realized the mistake. I was totally meaning to get you to the right spot—so my intentions were pretty high, and if it had been a real fire it definitely could have been a high-stakes mistake. But, because it wasn't a real fire, it ended up being a stretch mistake."

4. Explain that it is often easier to spot these mistakes first when you see someone else making them. So today the class is going to watch a short video where the characters make mistakes. The students will watch the video with the lens of spotting mistakes, then try to identify the type of mistake they see. "Keep an eye out for any mistakes you see. Then when you see one, look up at the chart and think about what type of mistake it could be."

5. Play the short film, stopping immediately following the first mistake made by a character, and then again at least once more immediately following a mistake, giving students a chance to share what they noticed and the type of mistake they believe they saw.

6. *Optional:* Ask students to think of a mistake from their mistakes boxes or résumés and see if they notice a pattern.

7. Close with letting students know that we all make all of these kinds of mistakes. But, as learners, we want more of our mistakes to be in the stretch area than anywhere else. However, it can be interesting to notice patterns of types of mistakes we tend to make and when. (Like making a lot of sloppy mistakes and hardly any stretch mistakes when we're tired.)

Lesson 8

HOW *NOT* TO REPEAT A MISTAKE

Grades: 3-12

Time needed: 10-15 minutes

Materials:

- A story of a mistake you made that you are willing to share with your students (This can be content specific or more social.)

- A chart or slide to show steps to follow

- Students sit with partner to talk with.

Lesson steps:

1. Begin by talking about how many of the mistakes we make are no big deal, or they are one-time events and so we are unlikely to repeat them. But there are other mistakes that we make that we very well could repeat and would rather not. You might say something like, "We make mistakes all the time. This might feel a little bit demoralizing, until we realize that most of our mistakes are actually no big deal or they're one-time things and we know we'll never repeat them again. However, occasionally, every once in awhile, we'll make a mistake that is a bit bigger

and there is a very real chance we could end up repeating that mistake because we know we'll be in that situation again. And those mistakes we would really rather not make again."

2. Ask students to discuss with a partner the best way to make sure to not repeat a mistake. You might say something like, "Today we're going to be talking about how to keep from repeating a mistake. I'd like you to tell someone sitting near you about one strategy you try when you just made a mistake that you don't want to repeat. This can be a mistake in school, with friends, maybe in sports or another activity you do."

3. After the students have talked, acknowledge that you, like many of them, thought that one of the best ways to not make a mistake again is to study it and spend a lot of time reflecting on it, maybe even writing about it.

4. Explain that mistake experts actually believe the better option is to only spend a short time thinking about a mistake (more if there is someone you need to make amends to). "Mistake researchers think that although it's a good idea to spend a little time, maybe a few minutes, on reflecting on a mistake, especially if you hurt someone else, you shouldn't spend too much time. Like, I know I often make a mistake and can think about it for a long time, all the ways I could have done it differently. Sometimes I can't sleep because I'm thinking so much about it. But experts don't think that keeps us from making the mistake again."

5. Pivot to explaining what can really work in keeping from repeating a mistake: spending a lot of time thinking of what your big values or goals are that the mistake got in the way of. I might say, "However, instead I can spend time thinking of the things I really value or my big goals that the mistake got in the way of. So, let's say I was late to someone's birthday party. I would

think about what my big value or goal was that lateness messed up. Like, being respectful to others or being a good friend. And I would spend some time thinking about just that value or goal and things I can do to make that value or goal happen."

6. Discuss how by focusing on the big picture your mind immediately starts to revise behaviors to focus on those values or goals, whereas when we spend too much time perseverating on a mistake, our brain remembers it too much and is more likely to repeat it. "It seems funny at first because we are so used to spending so much time thinking about the mistake itself. But when we do that, we're almost imprinting the mistake in our minds and making it more likely we'll repeat it. Instead, when we focus on goals and values, our brain already starts to plan how to get there."

7. Introduce the chart and discuss the steps:

> **One Strategy for Not Repeating the Same Mistake**
>
> - Notice that a mistake is something you've done before or you think you might do again.
>
> - Make sure you made amends with anyone who was negatively affected by the mistake.
>
> - Spend a few minutes thinking about what caused the mistake.
>
> - Think of what bigger goal (winning the championship, having specific responsibilities) or value (being kind, being a good friend) that the mistake got in the way of.
>
> - Spend some time thinking of ways you can better make sure that goal or value is a part of your life.

8. Talk about your mistake and take it through the steps. If this mistake is about a specific discipline, this is a great time to tuck in content.

9. Ask students to think of a low-risk mistake they don't mind sharing to practice trying to follow the steps so as to not repeat it. Use their partner to bounce ideas off of.

10. Encourage students to consider trying these steps the next time they make a mistake they'd rather not repeat.

Epilogue

It's What We Do Next That Matters

I've been thinking a lot about medicine lately.

The year 2020 is the sixty-fifth anniversary of the polio vaccine. Our nation's health care system has never been under greater scrutiny. And as I finish this book I am quarantined in my home in Brooklyn. New York City is the epicenter of a global pandemic. It is impossible to know what the world will look like by the time you read this book. Social mores, education, and commerce have upended, and it is difficult for me to imagine what will look the same and what will be different when or if the social distancing orders are over and the virus contained.

But I do know this: becoming a student of mistakes has greatly impacted how I view people's actions during the pandemic. We can see all the responses to mistakes discussed in this book—fear, disengagement ("everything will be OK"), denying equity issues, maintaining the status quo in illogical ways. Some have risked their own and others' lives distracted by the partisan arguments around COVID-19. We've seen inadequate local and national preparation for surges in infection rates . . . mistakes have been plentiful in this crisis, as is true in any crisis.

Searching for meaning in this chaos, I, like many Americans, was riveted by the words of Dr. Anthony Fauci. My attention was maintained by trust: here appeared to be an expert who is unafraid to acknowledge what he doesn't know. Many times people have tried to get him to say something soothing and calming but he consistently avoided false assurances by owning that not everything was known. Not everything was possible, no matter what so many of us wished for. There are no doubt criticisms that could be made, but his willingness to eschew empty comfort was something I respected.

And through it all I have watched in awe as educators across the world have figured out ways to embrace imperfection. You and so many other teachers have been inundated with your own and others' mistakes and have kept returning to what matters most, despite the chaos of new tools, faulty Wi-Fi, daily changing expectations, problems with student engagement and trauma. I watched as teachers struggled but adapted in ways that supported students and their families. Mistakes were made, undoubtedly. But these were often the very best kind—the ones made because educators and families were reaching past their own comfort zones, taking risks, and learning exponentially, alongside their students, in the process. And, my guess is, you haven't always been perfect, smiling, patient, organized angels of all that is good and right about education. There have been times things have been messy. You might even have shed a tear or two. Perhaps a cranky moment was had. Mistakes were made.

And it is precisely these mistakes that lead to great and earth-shaking innovations. One school in Queens was so concerned about students not having supplies for learning after schools were closed without warning, the teachers put out bins near the daily meal pickup spot so students could grab what they needed: book baggies, paper, crayons, dice, and even mealworms for the kindergartners to study at home. I've seen a teacher create short feedback videos recorded in her car on student reading reflections ("You've got me thinking" and "You've got me wondering") to replace the live reading conferences in a virtual learning environment. Teachers noticed that kids were looking disconnected and so moved to start every day with a virtual morning meeting, with some kids on video, some on phones; each day before the teaching begins, teachers said every child's name and "It's so good to see you!" Special educators pulled small groups of students in virtual hangouts, saw that students needed concrete examples and not pdf worksheets, and asked kids to grab paper plates, socks, and Legos to teach fractions. One teacher realized her written feedback inside of Docs was going unread and unnoticed, so she replaced it with recorded audio feedback and saw her students' responsiveness soar. A high school teacher noticed that attendance was low and so dropped the planned curriculum and taught students how to do real-time pandemic research and media criticism.

None of these are perfect. They don't have to be because they're focused on the most important thing: moving our values forward. This imperfect but crucial struggle makes me think of Alexander Fleming and his messy lab and cranky ways that led to a spore landing in a petri dish—which led to the discovery of penicillium. Without Fleming's cranky, messy mistake, penicillin might never have been discovered.

When we step in front of students again to teach, whether after the pandemic or on a rough Tuesday riddled with mistakes, let's try to remember that a mistake is just an action that went differently than we or our students intended. Every action can be followed up by another action. The mistake is not the key. It is important. It gives us that insight into knowledge and abilities we wouldn't have otherwise. But what is truly important is the next action after the mistake.

A closer look at the petri dish.

An erased answer replaced with a fresh attempt.

A smile and the words, "That happens to all of us. It's what we do next that matters."

IT IS PRECISELY THESE MISTAKES THAT LEAD TO GREAT AND EARTH-SHAKING INNOVATIONS.

Bibliography

ABC Education. 2011. "Learning from Design 'Mistakes.'" http://education.abc.net.au /home/-/m/1497009/L165/home#!/media/1575277/learning-from-design-mistakes-.

Adler, Gerhard, Michael Fordham, and Herbert Read, eds. 1973. *The Collected Works of C.G. Jung.* New York: Routledge.

Ahmed, Sara. 2018. *Being the Change: Lessons and Strategies to Teach Social Comprehension.* Portsmouth, NH: Heinemann.

Akasegawa, Genpei. 2010. *Hyperart: Thomasson.* Los Angeles: Kaya Press.

American Friends Service Committee. 1955. *Speak Truth to Power: A Quaker Study of International Conflict.* Pendle Hill Pamphlet. Philadelphia: American Friends Service Committee.

Arcade, Penny. 2016. "Longing Lasts Longer." Live performance, St. Ann's Warehouse, Brooklyn, NY.

Beck, Judith S. 2011. *Cognitive Behavior Therapy: Basics and Beyond.* New York: Guilford Press.

Becker, Shelly. 2018. *Even Superheroes Make Mistakes.* New York: Children's Sterling Books.

Bennett, Sara, and Nancy Kalish. 2007. *The Case Against Homework: How Homework Is Hurting Our Children and What We Can Do About It.* New York: Penguin.

Berkes, Howard. 2012. "Remembering Roger Boisjoly: He Tried to Stop Shuttle Challenger Launch." The Two-Way, February 6. *All Things Considered.* NPR. https:// www.npr.org/sections/thetwo-way/2012/02/06/146490064/remembering-roger -boisjoly-he-tried-to-stop-shuttle-challenger-launch.

Bhattacharjee, Yudhijit. 2017. "Why We Lie: The Science Behind Our Deceptive Ways." *National Geographic* (June).

Bloomquist, Ryan. 2016. "Patti LaBelle: 'Where Are My Background Singers?'" YouTube, October 23. https://www.youtube.com/watch?v=z84QdJlPpHE.

Briceño, Eduardo. 2015a. "Mistakes Are Not All Created Equal." Mindset Works, January 16. https://blog.mindsetworks.com/entry/mistakes-are-not-all-created-equal.

———. 2015b. "Why Understanding These Four Types of Mistakes Can Help Us Learn." KQED. https://www.kqed.org/mindshift/42874/why-understanding-these-four -types-of-mistakes-can-help-us-learn.

———. 2016. "How to Get Better at the Things You Care About." TED talk. https://www .youtube.com/watch?v=lGpAfX7Je7w.

Bronson, Po. 2008. "Learning to Lie?" *New York Magazine*, February 8. https://nymag .com/news/features/43893/.

Byrne, John. 2012. *Writing Comedy*, 4th ed. London, UK: Bloomsbury.

Calkins, Lucy. 2020. *Teaching Writing*. Portsmouth, NH: Heinemann.

Campbell, Joseph, with Bill Moyers. 1988. *The Power of Myth*. New York: Doubleday.

Canadian Observatory on Homelessness. 2019. "Reclaiming Power and Place: The Final Report of the National Inquiry into Missing and Murdered Indigenous Women and Girls." Toronto, ON: Canadian Observatory on Homelessness. https://www.mmiwg -ffada.ca/wp-content/uploads/2019/06/Final_Report_Vol_1a.pdf.

The Centre for Justice & Reconciliation. http://restorativejustice.org/#sthash.ODLT xEX2.1NeE2Bq3.dpbs.

Clasen, Mathias. 2017. *Why Horror Seduces*. New York: Oxford University Press.

Cohen, Steve. 2009. *Win the Crowd: Unlock the Secrets of Influence, Charisma, and Showmanship*. New York: HarperCollins.

Cooper, Harris, Jorgianne Civey Robinson, and Erika Patall. 2006. "Does Homework Improve Academic Achievement? A Synthesis of Research 1987–2003." *Review of Educational Research* 76 (1): 1–62. https://doi.org/10.3102/00346543076001001.

CROWN Coalition. 2019. Creating a Respectful and Open World for Natural Hair. https:// www.thecrownact.com/home.

Cruz, M. Colleen. 2015. *Unstoppable Writing Teacher: Real Strategies for the Real Class- room*. Portsmouth, NH: Heinemann.

DeGruy, Joy. 2017. *Post Traumatic Slave Syndrome: America's Legacy of Enduring In- jury and Healing*. Portland, OR: Joy DeGruy Publications.

"Education Resources for Schools Teachers and Students—ABC Education." 2020. Splash. Accessed April 15, 2020. https://education.abc.net.au/home/-/m/1497009 /L165/home.

Elbow, Peter. 2008. "The Believing Game—Methodological Believing." *The Journal of the Assembly for Expanded Perspectives on Learning* 14 (5). https://scholarworks.umass .edu/eng_faculty_pubs/5.

Ellis, Albert. 1997. *The Practice of Rational Emotive Behavior Therapy*. New York: Springer.

Firth, Jeremy, and Eduardo Briceño. 2017. "Learning and Performance Zones in Sports." Mindset Works, April 7. http://blog.mindsetworks.com/entry/learning-and -performance-zones-in-sports-2.

Fivush, Robin, Jennifer G. Bohanek, and Marshall Duke. 2008. "The Intergenerational Self: Subjective Perspective and Family History." In *Self Continuity: Individual and Collective Perspectives*, edited by F. Sani, 131–43. New York: Psychology Press.

France, Lisa Respers. 2020. "Deandre Arnold Heading to Oscars Thanks to 'Hair Love.'" CNN, January 31. https://www.cnn.com/2020/01/31/entertainment/deandre-arnold -hair-love-oscars/index.html.

Freeland, Claire A. B., and Jacqueline B. Toner. 2015. *What to Do When Mistakes Make You Quake: A Kid's Guide to Accepting Imperfection*. Washington, DC: Magination Press.

Gardner, Daniel. 2008. *The Science of Fear*. New York: Dutton.

Gee, James Paul. 2007. *What Video Games Have to Teach Us About Learning and Literacy*. New York: St. Martin's Griffin.

González, Norma, Luis C. Moll, and Cathy Amanti, eds. 2005. *Funds of Knowledge: Theorizing Practices in Households, Communities, and Classrooms*. New York: Routledge.

Gordon, Karen Elizabeth. 1993. *The Deluxe Transitive Vampire: The Ultimate Handbook of Grammar for the Innocent, the Eager, and the Doomed*, rev. ed. New York: Pantheon.

Gray, Carol. 2015. *The New Social Story Book, 15th Anniversary Edition: Over 150 Social Stories That Teach Everyday Social Skills to Children and Adults with Autism and Their Peers*. Arlington, TX: Future Horizons.

Gray, Peter. 2012. "The Many Benefits for Kids of Playing Video Games." *Freedom to Learn* (blog), January 7. *Psychology Today*. https://www.psychologytoday.com/us /blog/freedom-learn/201201/the-many-benefits-kids-playing-video-games.

Griffith, Janelle. 2020. "Second Black Texas Teen Told by School to Cut Dreadlocks, According to His Mom." NBC News, January 27. https://www.nbcnews.com/news/us-news/second-teen-suspended-over-dreadlocks-texas-school-n1122261.

Haidt, Jonathan. 2003. *Elevation and the Positive Psychology of Morality*. Washington, DC: *American Psychological Association*. DOI:10.1037/10594-012.

Hall, Tracey, Anne Meyer, and David Rose, eds. 2012. *Universal Design for Learning in the Classroom*. New York: Guilford.

Hallinan, Joseph. 2009. *Why We Make Mistakes*. New York: Random House.

Hammond, Zaretta. 2015. *Culturally Responsive Teaching and the Brain*. Thousand Oaks, CA: Corwin.

Hatch, Rachel. 2018. "Re-Believing Peter Elbow: An English Class Meets a Legend." Illinois State University News, August 24. https://news.illinoisstate.edu/2018/08/re-believing-peter-elbow-an-english-class-meets-a-legend/.

Herrera, Tim. 2019a. "Do You Keep a Failure Résumé? Here's Why You Should Start." *New York Times*, February 3. https://www.nytimes.com/2019/02/03/smarter-living/failure-resume.html.

———. 2019b. "So You've Made a Huge Mistake. What Now?" *New York Times*, June 9. https://www.nytimes.com/2019/06/09/smarter-living/so-youve-made-a-huge-mistake-what-now.html.

Howard, Jaleel, Tanya Milner-McCall, and Tyrone Howard. 2020. *No More Teaching Without Positive Relationships*. Portsmouth, NH: Heinemann.

Jacobson, Rae. n.d. "How to Help Children Manage Fears." Child Mind Institute. https://childmind.org/article/help-children-manage-fears/.

Jazaieri, Hooria, Geshe Jinpa, Kelly McGonigal, Erika Rosenberg, Joel Finkelstein, Emiliana Simon-Thomas, Margaret Cullen, James Doty, James Gross, and Philippe Goldin. 2012. "Enhancing Compassion: A Randomized Controlled Trial of a Compassion Cultivation Training Program." *Journal of Happiness Studies* 14 (4): 1113–26.

Jones, Charlotte Foltz. 2016. *Mistakes That Worked: The World's Familiar Inventions and How They Came to Be*. New York: Delacorte Books for Young Readers.

Jung, Carl. 1973. *The Collected Works of C. G. Jung*. Princeton, NJ: Princeton University Press.

Kendi, Ibram X. 2016. *Stamped from the Beginning*. New York: Nation Books.

The King Center. 2019. "The King Philosophy." January 8, 2019. https://thekingcenter.org/king-philosophy/.

Kohn, Alfie. 2007. *The Homework Myth*. Philadelphia: First Da Capo.

Kluger, Jeffrey. 2019. *Disaster Strikes! The Most Dangerous Space Missions of All Time*. New York: Philomel Books.

Kralovec, Etta, and John Buell. 2000. *The End of Homework*. Boston: Beacon.

Ladson-Billings, Gloria. 2009. *The Dreamkeepers*. San Francisco: Jossey-Bass.

Lahey, Jessica. 2015. *The Gift of Failure*. New York: Harper.

Lee, Fiona, Amy Edmondson, Stefan Thomke, and Monica Worline. 2004. "The Mixed Effects of Inconsistency on Experimentation in Organizations." *Organization Science* 15 (3): 259–374.

Lefer, Diane. 1994. "Breaking the Rules on Story Structure." In *The Best Writing on Writing*, v. 1, ed. Jack Heffron. OH: Story Press.

Lukeman, Noah. 2007. *The Dash of Style: The Art and Mastery of Punctuation*. New York: W. W. Norton.

Luyken, Corinna. 2017. *The Book of Mistakes*. New York: Dial Books.

MacNeil, Janet, Mark Goldner, and Melissa London. 2017. *The Stories of Science*. Portsmouth, NH: Heinemann.

Menakem, Resmaa. 2017. *My Grandmother's Hands: Radicalized Trauma and the Pathway to Mending Our Hearts and Bodies*. Las Vegas: Central Recovery Press.

Meyer, Anne, David H. Rose, and David Gordon. 2016. *Universal Design for Learning: Theory and Practice*. Wakefield, MA: CAST Professional Publishing

Midwinter, Amy. 2015. "My Favorite No." YouTube, March 14. https://www.youtube.com /watch?v=srJWx7P6uLE. March 14, 2015.

Mills, Heidi. 2014. *Learning for Real*. Portsmouth, NH: Heinemann.

Mills, Heidi, Tim O'Keefe, Chris Hass, and Scott Johnson. 2014. "Changing Hearts, Minds, and Actions Through Collaborative Inquiry." *Language Arts* 92 (1): 36–51.

Minor, Cornelius. 2019. *We Got This*. Portsmouth, NH: Heinemann.

Morin, Amanda. 2019a. *Math Skills: What to Expect at Different Ages*. Understood.org. https://www.understood.org/en/learning-thinking-differences/signs-symptoms /age-by-age-learning-skills/math-skills-what-to-expect-at-different-ages.

———. 2019b. *Reading Skills: What to Expect at Different Ages*. Understood.org. https:// www.understood.org/en/learning-thinking-differences/signs-symptoms/age-by -age-learning-skills/reading-skills-what-to-expect-at-different-ages.

Morris, Ryan. 2019. "Why We Lie: The Science Behind Our Deceptive Ways." *National Geographic*, June 18. https://www.nationalgeographic.com/magazine/2017/06/lying-hoax-false-fibs-science/.

National Sleep Foundation. n.d. "Why Do We Need Sleep?" https://www.sleepfoundation.org/articles/why-do-we-need-sleep.

NBC News Chicago. 2019. "'I'm Speechless': Emotional Albert Almora Jr. Reacts After Foul Ball Strikes Young Fan." https://www.nbcchicago.com/news/sports/chicago-baseball/chicago-cubs-albert-almora-emotional-foul-ball-hits-girl/158700/.

PBS Kids. 1987. "Talks About Making Mistakes." *Mister Rogers' Neighborhood*, May 6. Episode 1578. https://pbskids.org/video/mister-rogers/1421146807.

Peltz, Jack, Ronald Rogge, Heidi Connolly, and Thomas O'Connor. 2017. "A Process-Oriented Model Linking Adolescents' Sleep Hygiene and Psychological Functioning." *Sleep Health* 3 (6): 465–71. http://dx.doi.org/10.1016/j.sleh.2017.08.003.

Resnick, Mitchel. 2017. *Lifelong Kindergarten*. Cambridge, MA: MIT Press.

Richtel, Matt. 2016. "It's No Accident. Advocates Want to Speak of Car 'Crashes' Instead." *New York Times*, May 22. https://www.nytimes.com/2016/05/23/science/its-no-accident-advocates-want-to-speak-of-car-crashes-instead.html.

Romano, Aja. 2019. "Why We Can't Stop Fighting About Cancel Culture." *Vox*, December 30. https://www.vox.com/culture/2019/12/30/20879720/what-is-cancel-culture-explained-history-debate.

Rose, Todd. 2016. "How the Idea of a 'Normal' Person Got Invented." *The Atlantic*. February 18. https://www.theatlantic.com/business/archive/2016/02/the-invention-of-the-normal-person/463365/.

Rosser, James C. Jr., Paul J. Lynch, Laurie Cuddihy, Douglas A. Gentile, Jonathan Klonsky, and Ronald Merrell. 2007. "The Impact of Video Games on Training Surgeons in the 21st Century." *Archives of Surgery* 142 (2): 181–86.

Sackstein, Starr. 2015. *Hack Assessment: 10 Ways to Go Gradeless in a Traditional Grades School*. Cleveland, OH: Times 10 Publications.

Saltzberg, Barney. 2010. *Beautiful Oops*. New York: Workman Press.

Schulz, Kathryn. 2011. *Being Wrong: Adventures in the Margin of Error*. London: Granta Books.

Seppälä, Emma. 2015. "Why Compassion Is a Better Managerial Tactic Than Toughness." *Harvard Business Review,* May 6.

Sims Bishop, Rudine. 1990. "Mirrors, Windows, and Sliding Glass Doors." *Perspectives: Choosing and Using Books for the Classroom* 6 (3).

Snack Attack. 2015. United States: Arc Productions, Metanoia Films.

Steptoe, Andrew, Jane Wardle, and Michael Marmot. 2005. "Positive Affect and Health-Related Neuroendocrine, Cardiovascular, and Inflammatory Processes." *Proceedings of the National Academy of Sciences* 102 (18): 6508–12.

Stevens, Alison Pearce. 2019. "Noticing Mistakes Boosts Learning." *Science News for Students*, December 3. https://www.sciencenewsforstudents.org/article/noticing -mistakes-boosts-learning.

Stipp, Karen, and Kyle Miller. 2016. "Self-Care as a Trauma-Informed Practice." *Social Work Today*, November 3. https://www.socialworktoday.com/archive/exc_1117.shtml.

Strunk, William Jr., and E. B. White. 1999. *The Elements of Style*, 4th ed. New York: Longman.

Tannenbaum, Melanie. 2013. "But I Didn't Mean It! Why It's So Hard to Prioritize Impacts over Intent." *PsySociety* (blog), October 14, Scientific American.com. https:// blogs.scientificamerican.com/psysociety/e2809cbut-i-didne28099t-mean-ite2809d -why-ite28099s-so-hard-to-prioritize-impacts-over-intents/.

Tatum, Alfred. 2009. *Reading for Their Life*. Portsmouth, NH: Heinemann.

Tatum, Beverly Daniel. 2017. *Why Are All the Black Kids Sitting Together in the Cafeteria?* 2nd ed. New York: Basic Books.

Tavris, Carol, and Elliot Aronson. 2015. *Mistakes Were Made (but Not by Me): Why We Justify Foolish Beliefs, Bad Decisions, and Hurtful Acts*. New York: Houghton Mifflin Harcourt.

Taylor, Kimberly Feltes, and Eric Braun. 2019. *How to Take the Ache Out of Mistakes*. Minneapolis: Free Spirit Publishing.

Tomlinson, Carol Ann. 2017. *How to Differentiate Instruction in Academically Diverse Classrooms*. Alexandria, VA: ASCD.

Uluru Statement from the Heart. 2017. https://ulurustatement.org/the-statement.

Understood Team. 2019. *Writing Skills: What to Expect at Different Ages*. Understood. org. https://www.understood.org/en/learning-thinking-differences/signs-symptoms /age-by-age-learning-skills/writing-skills-what-to-expect-at-different-ages.

U.S. Food and Drug Administration. 2005. *Food Defect Levels Handbook*. https://www .fda.gov/food/ingredients-additives-gras-packaging-guidance-documents-regulatory -information/food-defect-levels-handbook.

UTMB Newsroom. 2012. "Young Gamers Offer Insight to Teaching New Physicians Robotic Surgery." *UTMB Health*, November 16. Galveston, TX: The University of Texas Medical Branch. https://www.utmb.edu/newsroom/article8061.aspx.

Utt, Jamie. 2013. "Intent vs. Impact: Why Your Intentions Really Don't Matter." *Everyday Feminism*, July 30. https://everydayfeminism.com/2013/07/intentions-dont-really-matter/.

Van Der Klift, Emma, and Norman Kunc. 1994. "Hell-Bent on Helping." https://www.broadreachtraining.com/van-der-klift-kunc-hellbent-on-helping-benevolence-friendship-and-the-politics-of-help.

Velez, Mandy. 2018. "Teacher Helps Students Make Skin Color Paints Beyond Brown and Tan." Yahoo!life, August 29. https://www.yahoo.com/lifestyle/teacher-helps-students-make-skin-color-paints-beyond-brown-tan-190106436.html.

Weinstein, Bruce. 2009. *Is It Still Cheating If I Don't Get Caught?* New York: Flash Point.

Wender, Jessie. 2015. "Six Beautiful Mistakes Caught on Camera." National Geographic, April. https://www.nationalgeographic.com/photography/proof/2016/04/01/april-fools-six-images-of-mistakes-gone-right/.

Widodo, Aemilia. 2016. "CGI Animated Short Film HD 'Last Shot.'" CG MeetUp. YouTube, July 28. https://www.youtube.com/watch?v=TYCFxvU-Lzg.

Wilson, Timothy D. 2015. *Redirect: Changing the Stories We Live By.* Boston: Back Bay Books.

World Health Organization. 2019. "Self-Care Can Be an Effective Part of National Health Care Systems." https://www.who.int/reproductivehealth/self-care-national-health-systems/en/.

Yeatts, Tabatha, ed. 2018. *Imperfect: Poems About Mistakes—An Anthology for Middle Schoolers.* History House Publishers.